ENSLAVEMENT *in* Memphis

ENSLAVEMENT *in* Memphis

G. WAYNE DOWDY

Published by The History Press
Charleston, SC
www.historypress.com

All images courtesy the Memphis and Shelby County Room, Memphis Public Libraries.

First published 2021

Manufactured in the United States

ISBN 9781467150149

Library of Congress Control Number: 2021938368

Notice: The information in this book is true and complete to the best of our knowledge. It is offered without guarantee on the part of the author or The History Press. The author and The History Press disclaim all liability in connection with the use of this book.

CONTENTS

AUTHOR'S NOTE

I dedicate this book to my late parents, Barbara Ann Nance and Gerald McLain Dowdy; my late grandparents, John McLain and Ivy Lucile Heckle Dowdy and William Herbert and Lurline Bell Griffin Nance; my uncles Larry and Ron Nance; and my beloved nieces and nephews Britney Amber Dowdy Pierce, Larry Hank Pierce, Mallorie Ann Pierce, Cody Austin Dowdy, Farrah Dawn Dowdy, Lawton Ryan Dowdy, Evan Caruso, Brandon Ryan Dowdy and Jessica Dowdy.

I also wish to thank my colleagues in the History and Social Sciences Department at the Benjamin L. Hooks Central Library—Gina Cordell, Robert Cruthirds, Scott Healy, Verjeana Hunt, Scott Lillard, SeCoya McNeil, Bonnie Pinkston, Leigh Ann Scarbrough, Marilyn Umfrees and Cindy Wolff—for their friendship and encouragement. The History Press is a wonderful publisher to write for, and I thank everyone there for their support, especially Senior Acquisitions Editor Chad Road. And finally, I wish to thank Gina Cordell, Paul Gahn, my godson Ellis Nelson Cordell Gahn, Carey, Beena, Natacha, Mischa, Dennis White, Derrick E. Patterson and Peyton Dubose.

Prologue

"NOTHING BUT CRUEL ABUSE, FROM MORNING TILL NIGHT"

Born a slave in North Carolina, Henry Davidson was a young boy in 1826 when brought to Memphis by his owner, Thomas P. Davidson, a Methodist circuit-riding preacher who became one of the city's most respected religious leaders before the Civil War. A kindly man who suffered from a lame leg, Thomas P. offered the basement of Wesley Chapel for slaves to hold worship services in 1841. Henry played a crucial role in the formation of both Wesley Chapel and its slave church service. Thomas P. apparently treated him more as a colleague and family member, and Henry was viewed by many whites as a co-founder of the city's Methodist church. However, Henry remained powerless to control his own fate and was subject to brutality, although it appears to never have been employed against him. Like his owner, Henry suffered from a disability. Unable to speak, Henry developed his own sign language, which greatly impressed his owner and fellow slaves. By the time of the Civil War, Henry Davidson was one of the most respected slaves in Memphis.

Life was far different for Louis Hughes. Born in Virginia to a white father and slave mother, when he was six years old, his paternal family sold him along with his mother and two brothers to a local physician. When the doctor died, they were sold to a merchant who hired Louis out to work on a canalboat. Told to gather his things, Louis went to his mother, who, "when she had made ready my bundle, she bade me good-bye with tears in her eyes she said 'son, be a good boy; be polite to everyone and always behave yourself properly.'" When he arrived in Richmond, Hughes discovered he

Slaves loaded and unloaded flatboats at the city's first wharf, seen here in 1830.

had been duped. A slave trader approached the twelve-year-old boy and said, "Your master sent you down here to be sold." Haunted by the memory of his mother, Louis endured being bought and sold several times until he was purchased by Edmund McGee of Pontotoc, Mississippi, as a Christmas gift for his wife, Sarah. Trained as a house servant, Louis was often whipped "for nothing, just to please my mistress' fancy." In 1850, Louis moved with the McGees to Memphis, where he helped build a palatial home on fourteen acres of land. Looking back on those days, Louis wrote, "In the new home my duties were harder than ever. The McGees held me with tighter grip, and it was nothing but cruel abuse, from morning till night."

Caroline, who was owned by the estate of Robert B. Daniel, faced a different kind of cruelty. In January 1846, she was hired out to Wilson Sanderlin to cook and wash clothes at his mill in rural Shelby County. Later that year, Caroline gave birth, and as a result, she and her child were sent to Memphis, where she was hired to work for a white family. Sadly, the child soon died, and Caroline was forced to keep working instead of being given time to mourn her loss. The same year Caroline began her work at Sanderlin's Mill, D.E. "Little Dan" Johnson was born in the home of Dr. A.P. Merrill, located at the intersection of Madison Avenue and North Second Street near the alley now called November 6 Street. His father, Dan, baked bread and cakes for the Merrills, and his mother, Margaret, washed clothes for the family. On her deathbed in 1857, Margaret asked Pat and Harriet Johnson, free persons of color living at the corner of Monroe and Third, to take care of her son. Little Dan wrote, "The Johnson's cared for me and my little sister, Maggie, for several years by permission of our master."

About the time Johnson was born, Mary Herndon of Missouri was sold to slave trader Nathan Bedford Forrest and brought to Memphis aboard a steamboat with one hundred other slaves. Arriving on the Fourth of July, Mary saw "lots of white men, all drunk, some fightin' and some standin' about in front of saloons....We was all taken to the n----r house, a long shed, divided and built on each side of a big yard. There we was kept until in the late fall." Sold to Louis Fortner of nearby Mason, Tennessee, Mary was put to work in the field, where she "chopped cotton, plowed it and did everything any other slave done."

The legacy of slavery, and the racism used to justify its existence, continues to weigh heavily on our society. There are many reasons for this, but one of the most pernicious is our refusal to accept the truth of slavery's barbarity and reconcile it with our belief that all humans are created equal. It is hoped that this book will, in a small way, help us achieve a better understanding of our shared past and assist us in creating a better future.

Chapter 1

"A LIKELY NEGRO GIRL"

1820–1835

When Memphis was founded in 1819, it was a lonely outpost of American slavery. Enslavement had begun over two centuries before when African slaves were brought to Spanish Florida in the 1560s, and British settlers in Virginia purchased twenty Africans from a Dutch ship captain some sixty years later. By the time colonial America revolted against the Crown and Parliament in 1776, slavery existed in every colony and was an important part of the new nation's economy. However, slavery was a thorny issue for white British subjects who screamed for liberty while denying it to others. A condemnation of British slavery was removed from the final draft of the Declaration of Independence lest it anger those who profited from it. Despite this, there were those revolutionaries who understood this glaring inconsistency and pointed it out. One signer of the Declaration of Independence, Dr. Benjamin Rush, wrote, "It would be useless for us to denounce the servitude to which the Parliament of Great Britain wishes to reduce us, while we continue to keep our fellow creatures in slavery just because their color is different from ours." In a nod to growing antislavery sentiment, Congress passed the Northwest Ordinance in 1787, which prohibited slavery in territories east of the Mississippi River and north of the Ohio River. However, there was much more proslavery sentiment in the United States than not.

The Constitution, which was ratified two years later, allowed slaveholding states to add three-fifths of their slave population to count their overall population when choosing representation in Congress. It also required that when runaway slaves crossed state lines, they were to be surrendered to their owners, and it gave Congress the power to end the external slave trade after 1808. At the same time, northern states abandoned slavery while it grew stronger in the South. A balance of power between the two regions was maintained as an equal number of new free and slave states entered the Union. However, in 1819, this delicate balance was upset when the Missouri Territory applied for statehood. Slavery already existed in the territory, which meant that if statehood was adopted, there would be one more slave than free state in the Union. Congress debated the issue for several months before adopting a compromise introduced by Illinois senator Jesse Thomas that brought Missouri into the United States as a slave state while recognizing part of Massachusetts as the new state of Maine. The law also established Missouri's southern border as the line between slave and free territory. The Missouri Compromise settled the question of slavery for the time being, but it almost guaranteed that the issue would continue to fester.

Six years before Henry Davidson arrived in Memphis, there were 103 slaves living and working in the city. Their names are known only to providence, as is the work they did. However, given the general nature of the early Memphis economy, we can speculate. More than likely most of them

There were 103 slaves in Memphis when it was founded in 1819.

worked on flatboats and the wharf, loading and unloading goods. Others worked in homes and saloons, and a few were blacksmiths, carpenters and woodchoppers. In 1826, Patrick "Paddy" Meagher opened the Bell Tavern on the east side of Front Street, where he provided food, shelter and firewood to riverboats and their workers. No doubt his slaves cooked, chopped firewood and did everything else required to serve Meagher's customers. Memphis was little more than a frontier outpost in the 1820s, a situation that afforded slaves the opportunity to flee their cruel servitude. On October 26, 1827, two of Meagher's slaves, Crese and Pleasant, fled the Bell Tavern for points unknown. Crese was described as "a likely negro girl, aged about sixteen years, with nose inclined to Roman. She has the ends from the third and fourth fingers of the right hand taken off by a burn and is extremely forward and pert when spoken to." In the same newspaper advertisement, Pleasant was described as "a negro man aged about 30 years, of common size and pretty well built; is soft spoken, but somewhat impudent when in liquor, to which he is addicted on some occasions, dresses fine, and with more than ordinary neatness, which gives an air of consequence which he does not commonly assume."

Ned, who was "about twenty two or three years of age; five feet nine or ten inches high; stout built; inclined to swing in walking; short face, with the hair of his head growing near his eye brows; he has a remarkable scar behind his left shoulder blade," labored on the farm of Joseph Graham and ran away on December 1, 1827. Two years later, Peter left Phoebus and Carr. Slaves not only ran away from Memphis, they also traveled to the city in hopes of escaping the South. In September 1827, a fourteen-year-old mulatto named Henry was taken from Nashville by his owner, Mr. Dunaway, to Flour Island Bluff, where he planned to sell him. Henry ran away and made it as far as Big Creek in rural Shelby County before being apprehended. The arrest of Henry is revealing for two reasons. First, we learn that despite the lack of law enforcement or organized slave patrols, whites were on the lookout for runaway slaves, and second, slaves from the surrounding region saw Memphis as a way station to freedom.

Slaves were also bought and sold in Memphis during the 1820s. The first recorded slave sale in Shelby County took place in 1820, when a Mr. Irvine sold a young man to Jacob Bean for $100. That same year, Thomas Lorance died, leaving an estate that contained "six kegs of corn whisky, three male slaves, a horse and saddle, a rifle, two three-point blankets (slightly worn), five dozen cotton shirts, $6 in cash, two old pocket knives, two bells, one hatchet and a note for $35 signed by one John Ogden." A ten-year-old girl

SCENE ON THE MISSISSIPPI, AT MEMPHIS, TENNESSEE.

Mississippi River traffic improved Memphis's economy and strengthened the institution of slavery.

named Alice was sold to Britton Duke by her owner, William Nickels, on June 21, 1828, and Horace Mayweathers was sold in 1833 to a Memphis owner, where he worked as a dishwasher in a boardinghouse. Living in an urban center, even a small one like Memphis, afforded slaves limited freedom of movement. For Jack and seven of his compatriots, this situation provided a chance to commit crime, which led to their arrest for attempted murder and burglary in 1832.

Buying and selling an individual slave was legal under state law, but importing slaves for the express purpose of selling them, otherwise known as slave trading, was not. In 1812, seven years before Memphis was founded, the second session of the Tennessee General Assembly prohibited the importation of slaves to sell for five years. If the law was violated, county sheriffs were authorized to seize the chattel and sell them. Few cared about the law because slavery was not that important to the state's economy, and some Tennesseans were not entirely comfortable with the institution. In the fall of 1826, a slave trader named Oliver Simpson imported several Blacks into Giles County expressly to sell them. The Giles County sheriff seized the slaves and was preparing to sell them when a joint resolution passed both houses of the General Assembly and ordered him to stop. The resolution led to the adoption of a stricter law that removed the five-year limitation and permanently banned slave trading in Tennessee. While part of the overall economy, slavery was not central to the growth of Memphis in the 1820s and early 1830s. Because of this, white Memphians were not fully committed to the institution and were open to the possibility of slavery's eventual abolition. We can see this most clearly when a reformer arrived in Memphis with a plan to educate and emancipate slaves and then send them to Africa. Born in Scotland in 1795, Frances Wright chafed at societal restrictions on women as she sought a broad education normally reserved for men. When she became an adult, she and her sister Camilla traveled to the United States, where they were enthralled by American democracy and appalled by American slavery. In her 1821 book *Views of Society and Manners in America*, she wrote, "Never shall I forget the feelings with which I first looked down from the gallery of the hall assembled representatives of a free and sovereign nation," when she visited Congress. Wright devoted a good deal of space in her book to the institution of slavery. She falls within the false white view that black people were "inferior…not so much on account of complexion and feature, as from the greater laxity of their morals, they may be more properly said to constitute a distinct than a degraded race." Racial prejudice, slavery's ugly twin brother, was casually practiced by most white people, even someone as relatively progressive as Frances Wright.

However, she was different in that she also stated that "we have sufficient data upon which to ground the belief, that he may, in time, be rendered a useful member of society." Of course, Henry Davidson and the other slaves were already useful members of society even if white people did not recognize them as such. Returning to England armed with her "sufficient data," Wright laid plans to help African slaves escape their degradation. In 1825, she coauthored a pamphlet with English farmer George Flower titled *A Plan for the Gradual Abolition of Slavery in the United States, Without Danger of Loss to the Citizens of the South*. The plan called for the purchase of a large tract of land where slaves would work off their purchase price, learn a trade and thus be prepared for their eventual freedom.

Believing that "Tennessee is the best slave state in the Union," Wright requested an audience with its leading citizen, General Andrew Jackson, who was a well-known land speculator as well as a noted politician and military leader. Wright and Flower traveled to the general's home outside Nashville, where they outlined their plan and Jackson recommended land that he owned on the outskirts of Memphis in rural Shelby County. Leaving Nashville, Flower and Wright traveled "forty miles a day on horseback, through unbroken country, spending the night in cabins open to the air on all sides, or in the woods themselves, a bearskin for my bed, my saddle for my pillow," Wright later wrote. Soon after arriving in Memphis, she purchased 320 acres from Jackson's land agents William Lawrence and William A. Davis. The property was soon enlarged when Wright bought an additional 920 acres. Jeremiah Evarts, a missionary traveling through the Bluff City, commented on Wright's arrival: "The famous Miss Wright…is here…she has actually entered upon the plan of liberating slaves by means of their own labor; and that she has commenced an establishment…not many miles from this place." The first slaves arrived at the newly christened Nashoba Settlement in February 1826, and they were soon joined by Jukey and her daughters Delilah, Elvira, Harriett, Isabel, Maria and Violet, who made the arduous journey from South Carolina to Memphis with their owner, Robert Wilson.

By the spring, residents had planted an apple orchard, five acres of corn and two acres of cotton and housed sheep and cattle that had been shipped from Illinois. However, as the summer heat bore down on the seven field hands, work began to slow. Jukey was a house servant who had no experience with field work, and her children were too young to make a meaningful contribution. Meanwhile, Frances Wright contracted malaria, which further eroded the success of Nashoba. Once recovered, Wright left Shelby County for France. Things soon deteriorated with the founder gone. Slaves were threatened with whippings if they did not work harder, and one female

Scottish reformer Frances Wright founded Nashoba in 1826 to liberate "slaves by means of their own labor."

servant was nearly raped before others interceded. James Richardson, the man left in charge, paid little attention to what was happening. Instead, he spent most of his time with his slave concubine until he fled at the end of 1827. Wright returned to Nashoba the following winter, but by the spring, it was realized she could not run the settlement without substantial help, which was not forthcoming. Reluctantly, she left Memphis to work at Robert Dale Owen's utopian colony, New Harmony, in Indiana. The settlement remained in operation until Wright was able to send Nashoba's thirty-four liberated slaves to Haiti, where they were given land by the Haitian government.

Other slaves did not wait for white reformers to free them. Hannah, described as "40 years old, 5 feet 3 or 4 inches high, thick built, speaks low and but little, black complected, has a sulky appearance, bushy hair, and wore a blue domestic frock but had other clothes," joined with six other slaves in an escape from George M. Penn on September 16, 1835. Crossing the Mississippi River, two of the slaves drowned, and four others were apprehended in Arkansas. Hannah was the only one left, and Penn believed "she is most probably in Arkansas making her way up the river." Sandy, who "had the scald head which makes his hair very thin," ran away from Miles W. Goolsley on October 29, 1835. In his newspaper advertisement, Goolsley stated, "He will aim for Memphis or Randolph and endeavor to get on a boat going up the river." A few weeks later, Lewis also fled from Goolsley, who described him as "about 25 years old, about five feet high, pale black, appears very humble when spoken to, speaks low, had on homemade clothing." Goolsley had purchased him from John Polk in the Shelby County hamlet of Portersville, and he thought he might be hiding there or was moving up the river to a free state.

Meanwhile, the thought of emancipating slaves and sending them to the Caribbean or Africa, first planted in Tennessee by Frances Wright, took root, and many whites across the state wanted emancipation and colonization to become state law. In 1834, the Tennessee General Assembly organized a convention to amend the state's constitution, which led to elections across the state to choose delegates. In Memphis, three candidates emerged, and each was committed to the abolition of slavery. Charles Stuart was the most strident, declaring, "Emancipation should precede and colonization would readily follow." Mayor Isaac Rawlings, who stated that "no one could look upon slavery with greater abhorrence than himself," joined with former congressman Adam Alexander in pledging to support colonization before abolition. Alexander eked out a narrow victory and traveled to Nashville in May 1834. Abolitionists like Alexander had their proposals rebuffed,

In May 1834, white Memphians sent an antislavery delegate to the Tennessee Constitutional Convention.

and instead the convention embedded slavery in the constitution. Article 31 stated, "The General Assembly shall have no power to pass laws for the emancipation of slaves, without the consent of their owner or owners." This left little hope for Alice, Crese, Henry Davidson, Horace Mayweathers, Peter, Pleasant, Ned and the other slaves in Memphis. However, they never abandoned their fight to gain freedom and a measure of human dignity.

Chapter 2

"A SCAR ON EACH HAND"

1836–1849

In the early days of 1836, Bill, described as "about 25 years old, 5 feet six inches high, of very dark complexion, high forehead with some of his front teeth out, when spoken to he answers quickly and wears a smiling countenance, weighs about 100 pounds," was owned by Thomas Mackey, the executor of the estate of John Best, deceased. Presumably, Mackey was holding Bill until the estate required his sale. On January 10, 1836, Bill was stolen from Mackey and taken to some unknown destination. Bill's experience reveals how valuable slaves were becoming in Memphis. In 1830, the city's slave population had risen to 2,149, despite the ban on slave trading, because individual citizens were free to buy and sell slaves with no governmental interference. On June 1, 1836, a twelve- or thirteen-year-old mulatto named Jane—owned by Thomas Bowling, Robert Gee and Eliza Mason—was sold to Britton Duke. Seven days later, Eppy White sold Ceala to Britton Duke, and John W. Jones sold thirty slaves as the executor of Edward Ward's estate in October 1838. At the same time, auctioneers and commission merchants began buying and selling slaves to meet the growing demand. Most of these early slave traders did not have permanent storefronts; instead, they sold slaves in various public places such as hotels, public parks and saloons. In February and March 1846, auctioneer J.E. Phillips sold many slaves at the Commercial Hotel, including Alexander; twenty-five-year-old "excellent general hand" Annita; Charles; Elizabeth; twenty-two-year-old "good cook, washer, ironer, &c" Henrietta; Isaac; "useful servant 12 years old" Joe; five-year-old Luke; Malinda; two-year-

Several commission merchants had their offices in the Commercial Hotel, where they auctioned and sold slaves on the front steps of the building.

old Marguerite; "excellent general hand, 9 years old" Mary; "excellent general hand 30 years old" Rachel; and two-year-old Rozetta.

There was also an increased demand for hiring slaves for specific jobs. In March 1839, Michael Leonard was looking to hire twenty to thirty "strong able bodied negro men," to whom he promised to pay good wages every month for their term of service. The following year, F. Carpenter wanted to hire "a likely young Negro man" who was an experienced wagoner or field hand for the spring, summer and fall of 1840. In June of that year, Robertson Topp, owner of the Gayoso Hotel, looked to purchase or hire a female slave "who can be well recommended as a good cook and house servant." Two years later, in May 1842, Eastin Morris wanted to hire "two good wood choppers, for a month or two," and in September 1846, the steamer *Maringo* advertised for twelve to sixteen slaves to work as firemen who serviced the boiler that kept the boat moving. In November 1847, the *Memphis Eagle* newspaper hired a young slave to work in the printing office. Slaves often learned skills that made them highly valuable not only to their owners but also to the local economy as a whole. For example, Henry became "a No. 1 plasterer," while Bill, Henry Bond and Mat. Wardlaw were successful wagon drivers or draymen. Austin Cotton was a respected carpenter, and Thomas Bradshaw was trained as both a barber and musician. As a result of their value, skilled slaves were often treated better than their more disposable brethren. Thomas Bradshaw, for example, stated, "I am an old citizen here, and those who knew me treated me very well in the position I held." Although only a few skilled slaves can be identified, there is every reason to believe that the enslaved were involved in all major building projects of the 1830s and 1840s, including the Gayoso House hotel and restaurant and the United States Navy Yard. Meanwhile, the city's position on the river made it an ideal place for the movement of cotton from nearby farms and plantations to ports around the world. In 1830, one thousand bales worth \$3,500 were shipped from Memphis, and ten years later, thirty-five thousand bales valued at \$1,400,000 passed through the city. This made cotton the driving force behind the growth of slavery and the Memphis economy as textile mills in Europe and the United States demanded more and more product. As a result, many slaves worked on the levee, loading and unloading Mississippi River steamboats filled with what was often referred to as "white gold." This increased demand for labor led to an expansion of the local slave population. In 1830, there were 2,149 slaves in Memphis, and that number grew to 7,040 by 1840 and ten years later increased to 14,360 slaves.

In February 1826, Thomas P. Davidson, with Henry at his side, preached a sermon to the members of the First Methodist Society: Elijah Coffee, a Portuguese immigrant named Dickens and Pauline Perkins. Services were soon held in a log cabin near the mouth of the Wolf River and later moved

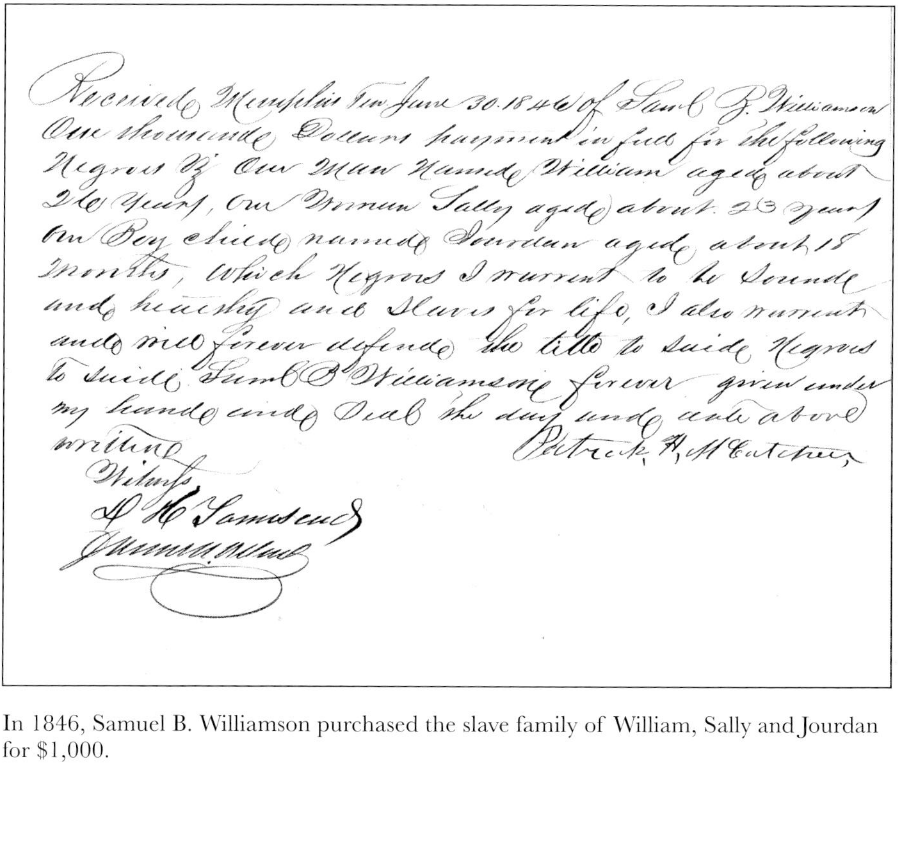

Received Memphis Tenn June 30. 1846 of Saml B. Williamson One thousand Dollars payment in full for the following Negroes Viz One Man Named William aged about 26 Years, One Woman Sally aged about 23 years One Boy child named Jourdan aged about 18 Months, Which Negroes I warrent to be Sound and healthy and Slaves for life, I also warrent and will forever defend the title to said Negroes to said Saml B Williamson forever given under my hand and Seal the day and date above written

Patrick H. McCutchen

Witness

A H Sampson

[illegible]

In 1846, Samuel B. Williamson purchased the slave family of William, Sally and Jourdan for \$1,000.

to the dining room of the Blue Ruin Tavern before a permanent structure was erected in 1832. Their first minister was the Reverend Francis A. Owen, who convinced the eleven members of the congregation to purchase a plot of land at the corner of Poplar Avenue and Second Street for $200. There they constructed a new church building called the Old Meeting House. As Owen expanded the congregation, Thomas P. and Henry established several Methodist missions in other parts of the city and county. Perhaps because of Henry, Thomas P. and Owen allowed slaves to attend services as long as they sat in the gallery. By 1843, the First Methodist Society had outgrown the Old Meeting House, so they completed a larger brick building in 1845, which they named Wesley Chapel. When the new building opened, the basement was deeded to the Wesley Chapel African Mission.

As the population increased, so did the number of slaves who sought a measure of freedom by running away from their owners. A forty-year-old slave named Mitch, who was six feet tall and rather heavy, fled from Lawrence H. Bedford on May 5, 1836. Durritt and Barnes had two of its slaves run away four months later: Isaac, "a very likely black fellow about twenty years of age, five feet six inches high, some small scars on his face," and Robert, "a likely yellow fellow, 21 or 22 years of age, about 5 feet ten inches high, has a scar on his right hand, occasioned by a burn…is very stout, weighs about 180 pounds." Some slaves adopted the guise of free people of color and changed their names. In 1839, Quicksel changed his name to Cato and used his soft speaking voice and "pleasing countenance" to escape from his owner. When John ran away from William Winfrey's farm in the Shelby County hamlet of Germantown, he put on his green frock coat and blue cloth pants to head for the free states. Along the way, he no doubt employed his "good manners" and skill at "telling extravagant tales" to avoid capture. Others were far more interested in being reunited with their families, like twenty-eight-year-old Cato, who donned his black fur hat to join his wife in the rural Shelby County town of Randolph. Jim ran away from Claiborne Barksdale, who described him as having "six toes on each foot with a scar on each hand caused by cutting one finger on each hand. Also a scar on one side of his face caused by a bite; a little inclined to be knock-kneed." Descriptions such as these clearly show the physical abuse many slaves experienced. Robert had a burn scar on his right hand, Isaac's face was scarred and Jim had his fingers cut and a scar on his face.

Slaves not only ran away from Memphis, but they also traveled to the city in hopes of using the Mississippi River as an avenue of escape. State law required county sheriffs to arrest runaways, advertise their incarceration

Wesley Chapel's Old Meeting House, where Henry Davidson worked and worshiped.

and hold them until claimed by an owner. If a slave was not claimed after one year, then the sheriff was authorized to sell him or her. Many of the slaves came from north Mississippi and west Tennessee. Jack came from LaGrange, Tennessee; Reuben ran away from Mr. Polk in Holly Springs, Mississippi; and Peter, described as "a boy about 40 or 45 years of age, 5 feet 3 or 4 inches high, weighs about 144 pounds, very black, little bald headed, a tooth out," fled Stephen Rutlan's farm in DeSoto County, Mississippi. From Wilkinson County, Mississippi, twenty-three-year-old George ran away from William White and was arrested in Shelby County, where he languished in jail for a year until he was sold to another owner. Runaways were not just men. A twenty- or twenty-two-year-old "very quick spoken and speaks somewhat broken" woman named Ann was arrested and housed in the Shelby County Jail on October 26, 1838, along with Amanda, a nineteen-year-old stoutly built mulatto.

Others came from much farther away. A twenty-five-year-old "yellow man" named William, who had one of his front teeth missing, made it all the way from Stanton, Virginia, before being arrested in Memphis. At least two arrested slaves came from New Orleans before being caught: Feildon, a twenty-eight-year-old dark-complexed man, ran away from a Mr. Ford, and

Slaves used Memphis's proximity to the Mississippi and Wolf Rivers to run away from their servitude.

John, a twenty-year-old who weighed 150 pounds and had a dark brown complexion, fled from a Mr. Kilpatrick. From Missouri, Thompson made his way to Shelby County, where he was arrested on September 18, 1838, and sold on October 7, 1839, when his owner, James Watson, failed to claim him. Shortly before Thompson was sold, the sheriff detained nineteen-year-old Abraham, who was owned by James Wall of Louisville, Kentucky. Even free persons of color were not immune from arrest. George Wise, a thirty-year-old free man from Allegheny County, Pennsylvania, was arrested by the Shelby County sheriff for being a runaway slave on May 22, 1839, and sold on July 6, 1840. It is not known how slaves were treated while in jail, but it is doubtful they simply laid around, waiting for their owners to come. A fascinating document from the pen of Sheriff John W. Fowler, who served from 1836 to 1842, gives us an idea of their treatment, at least while Fowler was sheriff. After leaving office, Fowler owned a large plantation in rural Shelby County. On August 25, 1859, he composed a set of rules governing how his slaves were to be treated:

> *Punishment must never be cruel or abusive for it is absolutely mean and unmanly to whip a negro from passion, malice, and any man who can do so, is utterly unworthy and unfit to have control of either man or beast. My negroes are all permitted to come to me with their complaints and grievances and in no instance shall they be punished for so doing…Prove and show by*

> *your conduct towards the negroes that you feel a kind and considerate regard for them. Never cruelly punish or overwork them. Never require them to do what they cannot reasonably accomplish, or otherwise abuse them, but seek to render their situation as comfortable and contented as possible.*

Some whites may have taken comfort in the benign nature of Fowler's rules, but slaves did not. Isaac, Jim, Robert and the rest of the slave population knew full well that their owner could someday give in to "passion" or "malice" and commit abuse, rape or even murder, and they had no power to stop him.

The growing number of slaves in Memphis led local government to take its first steps to control the population. On March 26, 1839, the board of aldermen passed an ordinance authorizing the hiring of two watchmen whose duties included arresting every slave "that he or they may find out after 10 o'clock, and lodge them in the calaboose…until next morning, (unless they have a special pass from their master or mistress), at which time, he, she or they, so arrested, shall receive ten lashes on their naked back…and a fine of two dollars be imposed on the owner of such slave or slaves." This law did little to curb the movement of runaways; they continued to hide in plain sight while using the river to escape their bondage. The watchmen no doubt thwarted slaves like Amanda, Ann and Reuben, but law enforcement

Slaves loading cotton bales onto a wagon in 1853.

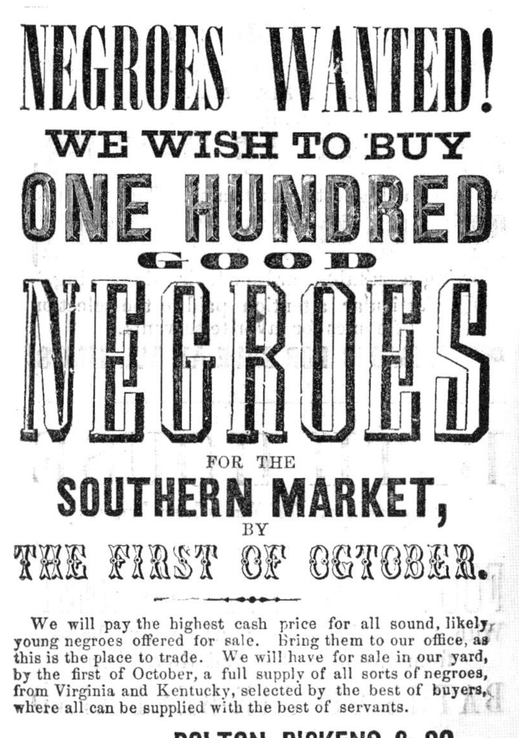
NEGROES WANTED!
WE WISH TO BUY
ONE HUNDRED
GOOD
NEGROES
FOR THE
SOUTHERN MARKET,
BY
THE FIRST OF OCTOBER.

We will pay the highest cash price for all sound, likely young negroes offered for sale. Bring them to our office, as this is the place to trade. We will have for sale in our yard, by the first of October, a full supply of all sorts of negroes, from Virginia and Kentucky, selected by the best of buyers, where all can be supplied with the best of servants.

BOLTON, DICKENS & CO.

MEMPHIS, TENN.

Founded in 1845, Bolton, Dickens and Co. was the first slave-trading company in Memphis.

also relied heavily on vigilant whites who were always on the lookout for out-of-place "Negroes." However, by the mid-1840s, the available evidence suggests that many whites no longer turned over runaways to the sheriff but instead sold them to willing buyers. We know this for two reasons—first, from 1845 jailors' notices that described newly incarcerated slaves disappeared from local newspapers, and second, that same year marked the establishment of the first fully functioning slave market in Memphis.

Late in 1845, Isaac L. Bolton and Tom Dickens defied state law in forming Bolton, Dickens and Co., the first slave-trading firm in Memphis. Their initial act was the purchase of eight-year-old Ann from W.L. Montgomery, which led to the buying and selling of many other slaves over the next few months. The firm quickly outgrew its modest offices, and they purchased a building on the north side of Adams Street for $1,600. Converting it into a slave market with detention cells, an office and a viewing area, it did not take long for Bolton, Dickens and Co. to become one of the wealthiest businesses in the Bluff City. Others took notice of their success, including Isaac's brother Wade, who was a well-known cotton merchant in the city. In the fall of 1846, Wade rented a building on the corner of Adams and Main Streets for his own slave market. Advertising in the December 2, 1846 edition of the *Memphis Appeal*, Wade Bolton declared, "I have for sale plenty of boys, men and women and some fancy girls. I intend to have a constant supply through the season and will not be undersold by any agent in this market. My motto is 'the swift penny; the slow shilling,' I will never get. I will also pay highest cash for young negroes." A year later, Wade joined Isaac to form a stronger Bolton, Dickens firm, which gave them the financial capital to dominate the slave trade in Memphis.

For Carolina, Davy, Gaston, George, Isaac Felder, Hannah Washington and the many others who were crowded into the dank, jail-like rooms in the Bolton, Dickens slave market, a new phase in the sorry tale of slavery in Memphis was just beginning as the 1840s came to an end.

Chapter 3

"NOTHING BUT THE DEVIL UP HERE"

1850–1859

When Louis Hughes arrived at his owner's palatial home in 1850, he was assigned the jobs of body servant to "Boss" Edward McGee and butler for the household. Each morning, he dusted the parlor and hallway and prepared the dining room for breakfast. Once he served the meal, Louis spent the rest of his day retrieving the mail, brushing his owners' clothes, washing windows and polishing the silver. Each day he wore a cloth suit modeled on those worn by New York waiters, which made him feel "light-hearted at this improvement in my personal appearance, although it was merely for the gratification of my master's pride; and I thought I would do all I could to please Boss." One morning as he worked arranging the parlor, Louis overheard "the Madam" Sarah McGee declare, "It don't do to praise servants." Heartbroken, his feelings began to harden toward his white owners as they meted out both mental and physical abuse. Mrs. McGee loved nothing more than to beat her slaves whenever she felt like it. One day, Louis finished cleaning the front steps when the Madam became enraged. Pushing Louis into the yard, she ripped off his shirt and beat him with a switch. Louis burst into tears, but then something changed. "The feeling came over me that I was a man, and it was an outrage to treat me so—to keep me under the lash day after day." Tired of the constant abuse, Louis began to think of ways to escape his torment. Ironically, it was his owner who first gave him the idea. Several times he overheard Boss and Madam discussing reports of slaves running away to Canada. Around the same time, Boss's father Old Master

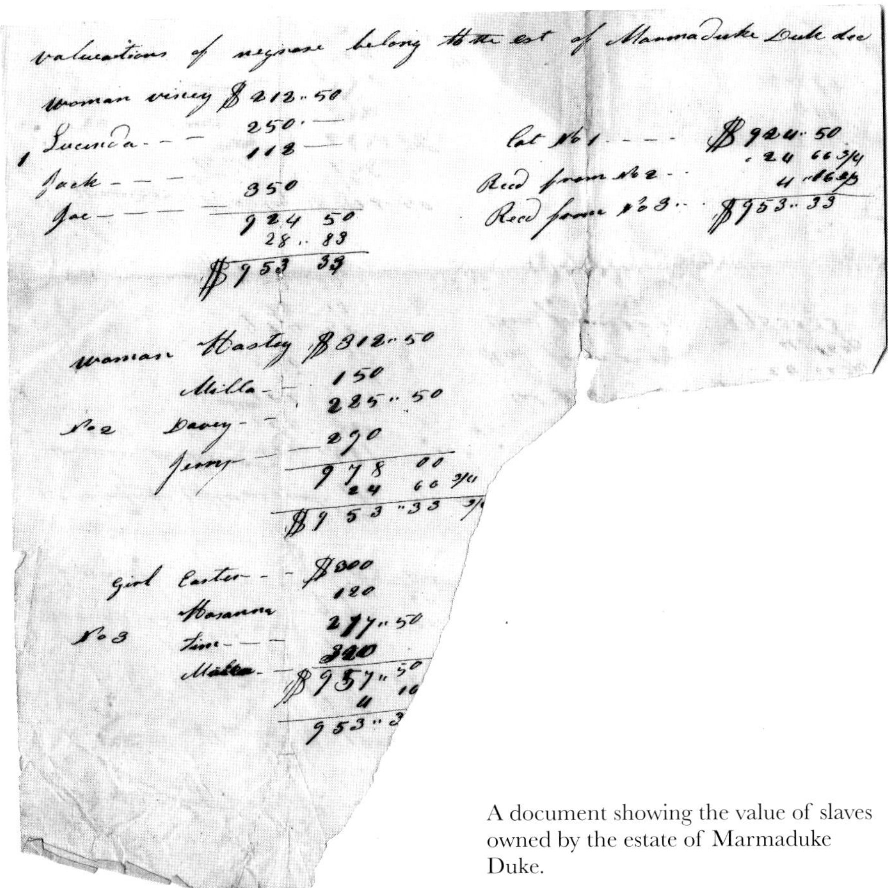

valuations of negroes belong to the est of Marmaduke Duke dec

woman vincy $212.50
Lucinda --- 250
112
Jack --- 350
Joe ---
924 50
28 .. 83
$953 33

Lot No 1 ---- $924.50
.24 66 3/4
Recd from No 2 .. 4 16 2/3
Recd from No 3 .. $953.33

woman Hasty $312.50
Milla --- 150
No 2 Davey --- 225.50
Jerry --- 290
978 00
24 66 3/4
$953.33 3/4

girl Easter --- $300
120
Harannu 277.50
No 3 Jim --- 320
Milla --- $957.50
4 16
953.3

A document showing the value of slaves owned by the estate of Marmaduke Duke.

Jack visited the new home, where he toured the grounds with Hughes and his son. Impressed with the stately home, Master Jack said, "Well, it's good, but I'm afraid you'll spoil these n----rs....Keep your eye on that boy Lou, he is slippery....I see running away in his eyes."

Other whites saw more than the desire for escape in the eyes of the enslaved. In particular, city government was concerned with the growing population of slaves and their relative freedom of movement. On March 27, 1850, the board of aldermen passed a bill that did not allow "slaves to remain in corporate limits of city after sun set or any part of the Sabbath, except by permission of owner specifying limit of time," or permit gatherings of slaves "except for public worship conducted in an orderly manner under superintendence of a white person." It also banned slaves from congregating in saloons and bars. In 1854, the aldermen passed another ordinance granting a reward for anyone, including police officers, who captured a runaway slave. Wanting to restrict hired slaves roaming the streets and collect additional revenue, the board of aldermen in 1858 levied a twenty-dollar tax on all slaves owned by non-residents who were employed or hired in the city.

Meanwhile, the McGees' cook, Delia, faced her own share of abuse. One morning, she and Louis heard Madam yelling loudly for Delia. Turning to Louis, she spit out, "Dah! I wonder what she wants now!" Red-faced, Madam entered the kitchen screaming, "What kind of biscuits were those you baked this week?" Quietly, Delia replied, "I think they were all right, Mis Sarh." "Hush!" Madam yelled. "You did not half cook them; they were not beat enough." "Well, Mis Sarh, I tried." Not pleased with Delia's response, Madam exclaimed, "Stop! I'll give you thunder if you dictate to me." Her anger dissipated, Madam stalked out of the kitchen. Turning to Louis, Delia said, "My Lord, that woman dunno what she wants. Ah, Lou, there is nothing but the devil up here; can't do nothin' to please her in this fine huse. I tell you Satan never git his own til he git her."

The hard work required of house servants could, in its own way, be just as dangerous as being subjected to a devilish owner. One evening, the maid Celia worked furiously sewing a garment to be worn on a trip scheduled for the following day. Well past midnight, she still hunched near a bright candle preparing the clothes. Celia's eyes became heavy as exhaustion crept up her spine and entered her brain. As she slept, the garment fell into the candle and caught fire. The flames quickly engulfed Celia, who screamed and ran down the hall in a vain attempt to escape the fire. Boss yelled for Louis, and the two attempted to smother the flames with water and a blanket. Sadly, they were too late to save Celia. "Poor girl, poor girl! She is burned to death," Boss exclaimed.

The loss of his mother, Madam's physical abuse and the gruesome death of Celia convinced Louis that if he wanted to live, his only option was to run away. One morning, Madam screamed for Louis to come into the house and receive a beating. Instead of following her order, Louis ran past the garden, through the woods and into downtown Memphis. At the city's wharf, he soon spied an unoccupied boat named the *Statesman*. Climbing aboard, he hid behind four hogsheads of sugar and prayed the boat would leave soon. As night drenched the river and its occupants, hunger and thirst gnawed at Louis, so he went in search of sustenance. He found the remains of a meal in the boat's kitchen, and after quickly eating, he slunk back to his hiding place. On the third night of his journey, he was discovered by the second mate, who took him to the captain. As he stood in the pilothouse,

Louis Hughes used steamboats like this one to unsuccessfully escape from Memphis.

Louis was bombarded with questions as the crew searched through a stack of newspapers. An advertisement Boss had composed was found and read out loud to Louis, the crew and a handful of passengers. "Ran away from Edmund McGee, my mulatto boy Louis, 5 feet 6 inches in height, black hair, is very bright and intelligent. Will give $500 for him alive, and half of this amount for knowledge that he has been killed."

"That's a bright boy to be a slave," the captain said. Turning to Louis, he asked him to dance for them. Louis obliged them, and when he finished, the captain asked the crew and passengers for donations, which netted Louis two dollars. The next night, they docked at West Franklin, Indiana, where a sympathetic passenger warned him to immediately flee the boat. Once ashore, his absence was noticed, and an alarm was sounded. Running through the small town, he made it into the woods before spying two men on horseback. They paid little attention to Louis, who made his way to a farmhouse where he was fed by an old woman and her daughter. While Louis was enjoying his meal, the two men arrived in town and discovered they had just passed a wanted man. Rushing back to the area, they soon were knocking on the kind woman's door. "There is a runaway n----r out, who stole off a boat this evening," they explained. Trembling with fright, Louis admitted to being the runaway in question. They took him into custody, and the next morning a trial was held to determine what was to be done with Louis. The law was fairly straightforward—the 1793 and 1850 Fugitive Slave Acts required federal judges and local magistrates to rule on the status of an alleged runaway slave and take the appropriate action. Hughes was brought before a magistrate in Louisville, Kentucky, who ruled that "Captain Montgomery brought forth a boy, and said he is the property of Edmund McGee of Memphis, Tenn. Come forth owner, and prove property, for after the boy shall remain in jail six months he shall be sold to pay jail feed."

It didn't take McGee long to arrive in Louisville. "Hello, Lou! What are you doing here, you dog?" McGee greeted the frightened Louis. When they returned to Memphis, Louis was surprised to learn he would not be whipped for running away. However, he sensed Madam's rage and knew she would not waste much time in having her revenge. "But after I had been home some three or four weeks, Madam Sarah commenced her old tricks—attempting to whip me, box my jaws and pinch me. If any little thing was not pleasing to her at mealtime, it was a special delight for her to reach out, when I drew near to her to pass something, and give me a blow with her hand," Louis remembered.

Three months later, he tried again. Boarding a mail packet from Cincinnati, Louis hid in the empty hull, which was soon filled with cotton bales. For two nights, he lay on top of the bales as the boat churned through the Mississippi. Deprived of fresh air, food and water, Louis stumbled out of the darkness and into the hands of a crewman who took him to the pilot house. When they arrived at Monroe, Kentucky, he was placed in the local jail until the packet's return voyage to Memphis. Arriving at one o'clock in the morning, Louis spent another night in jail until he was sent home. As they drove into the McGees' yard, Madam declared, "You put up at the wrong hotel, sir." Taken to the barn, he was placed into wooden stocks and his shirt was ripped from his body. Boss whipped him for two hours, "the terrible rawhide cutting into my flesh at every stroke," Louis later remembered. Peach tree switches that cracked and inflamed the whip scars and a wooden paddle to cause further pain were also used. When the beatings ended, salt and water were poured on Louis's raw flesh to wash the wounds. "God only knows what I suffered under it all, and He alone gave me strength to endure it. I could hardly move after the terrible ordeal was finished and could scarcely bear my clothes to touch me first, so sore was my whole body, and it was weeks before I was myself again."

The Mississippi River not only provided opportunities for escape; it was also the main artery for transporting enslaved people. James Gill was seven years old when his owner, Tom White, took him, his parents and several other slave families from Alabama to a new homestead in Phillips County, Arkansas. Gill's father was a skilled blacksmith and carpenter who was needed to construct buildings on the Arkansas property. With their white overseer Jim Lynch, Gill and his family boarded a train that took them to Memphis. "I got so scared 'cause I hadn't never seen no train before, and I just hollered and cried," Gill recalled. At Memphis, they were put on a steamboat that took them to Arkansas. Sam Barnett was brought from South Carolina by a slave trader who auctioned him in Memphis. When steamboats glided into Memphis, one of the first things they saw was a large sign that declared "Bolton, Dickens & Co., Slave Dealers." Located on Clinton Street, between Front Street and the river, the Bolton, Dickens slave mart was "one of the best prisons in the State, receiving daily large supplies of fresh negroes from the buying markets." The company soon expanded into St. Louis and Vicksburg, Mississippi, which led to the routine shipment of slaves from Memphis. In September 1856, for example, the company sold Daniel, Eudora, Harriett, Jenisalene, Mariah, Sedrick and Tom Bar to Saul Hawkins of Vicksburg. That same year, it sent Agnes Faro, Amanda Wood, Ben Bangor, Carolina Whaley, Tom, William and Woodson on the steamer *Princess* to G.L. Bumpass in Lexington. In January 1857, Aaron, Benjamin, Cherry, Ebenezer Jones, Frances, General Jackson, Harriett, Jack Johnson, Jennie, Joe McKitchen, Morning, Patsy, Robert Henry Lewis, Susan and Terry were sold to a dealer named Murfield. Bolton, Dickens catered to the upwardly mobile farmers and planters who were getting rich quick feeding the world's insatiable demand for cotton. As one advertisement put it:

> *Call and buy before the present stock is picked over, as some is of the opinion that the first show at a fresh lot is one hundred dollars the advantage—but we say to you the last will be good. So, call and make your purchases to gather your crop—and then call quick again and buy to make another crop. By those means if you will keep up your purchases for ten years there is no telling how much you may be worth. This is the true road to wealth and if you neglect the present offer of becoming wealthy it's your own fault and not ours as the road is laid out plainly.*

As some Memphians grew rich from cotton and trading, the city's general view of slavery evolved from slight unease to enthusiastic support. At the

Many slaves were sold in Court Square, seen here in the early twentieth century.

same time, state government abandoned enforcement of its 1826 law that forbade the interstate slave trade in Tennessee. The ordinance was widely ignored and, in 1853, finally repealed. Two years later, there were six slave dealers in Memphis: Bolton, Dickens and Co., Delap and Witherspoon, Byrd Hill and Son, Nevill and Cunningham, G.N. Noel and Forrest and Maples. This competition weakened Bolton, Dickens's position as the oldest and most successful slave-trading firm in Memphis. Then, to make matters worse, Isaac Bolton murdered a fellow trader over the fraudulent sale of a free Negro apprentice.

In the spring of 1857, Washington Bolton, who had joined the firm despite having no family connection to Isaac and Wade, visited Lexington, Kentucky; purchased a Black female indentured apprentice from James McMillan; and sent her to Memphis. She was sold to Parson David Crenshaw, but when her time expired, she informed the parson that she was free. Examining her papers, Crenshaw realized he had been cheated and filed suit against Bolton, Dickens. The suit could not have come at a worse time because the firm was nearly bankrupt. Forced by the courts to give Crenshaw his money back, Isaac seethed with uncontrolled anger. Unfortunately for him, McMillan arrived in Memphis at the end of May with a few slaves to sell. Wade Bolton saw McMillan on the street and asked him to bring a "fancy boy" to the mart for possible sale. Although reluctant to be near any Bolton, the lure of quick cash eased McMillan's fear. When he arrived at the Bolton, Dickens mart, he was met by Isaac, who cursed and threatened to kill him if he did not refund the money from the free Negro sale. When McMillan said he had no money, Isaac shot him dead. He lived long enough to tell a gathering crowd that Wade had lured him to the mart and Isaac killed him. Although their fortunes were waning, the Boltons had enough money left to hire excellent lawyers and bribe the jury, which led to their acquittal in 1858. The firm limped along until the Civil War began, but it never regained its former position as the most prosperous slave dealership in Memphis.

One of Bolton, Dickens's main rivals was the firm headed by Byrd Hill. In an advertisement published in the March 24, 1859 edition of the *Memphis Daily Appeal*, Hill declared in bold type:

> *If you want negroes, come to Memphis.*
>
> *Having permanently located myself in this Bluff City, with the advantage of many years' experience and close observation as to the wants of the people, and how those wants may be best supplied, I have therefore established a Negro Mart, on a basis more liberal and accommodating in its character than heretofore introduced in the South. I propose to always keep on hand an assortment of the Very Best Negroes that several markets afford, consisting of Men, Women, Boys, and Girls, to wit: Field Hands, Mechanics, Body Servants, Cooks, Washers, Seamstresses, Nurses, etc., all of which I will sell at Private Sale and at Auction.*

Meanwhile, Nathan Bedford Forrest, a mercantile and slave dealer from Hernando, Mississippi, arrived in Memphis during the spring of 1852 to partner in a new enterprise with a slave trader named S.S. Jones. On February 1, 1854, Forrest purchased a tract of land on Adams Street between Second and Third, behind Calvary Episcopal Church, that would become one of the largest slave markets in the city. He partnered with Josiah Maples in 1855, and the two increased the size of their market to include several buildings for housing slaves and a brick home for Forrest and his family. In the late 1850s, a five-year-old named Horatio J. Eden and his mother were brought to the Forrest slave market to be sold. In an interview conducted in 1923, Eden described how the market operated:

> *The yard, a kind of square stockade of high boards with two room Negro houses around, say a three sides of it and high board fence too high to be scaled, on the other side is sides. We were all kept in these rooms but when an auction was held or buyers came, we were brought out and paraded two or three around a circular brick walk in the center of the stockade. The buyers would stand nearby and inspect us as we went by, stop us and examine us.*

Mary Herndon's experience was similar to Eden's. Born in Indian Territory, she was brought by her first owner to Cameron, Missouri, where she nursed children and became a "sewing girl." When her owner's property was seized by the sheriff for nonpayment of debts, she was sold to Forrest along with many other slaves. Herndon and her fellow slaves were transported by wagons to St. Louis and then sent by steamboat to Memphis. In a 1933 interview, Herndon remembered that "we was all taken to the n----r house, a long shed, divided and built on each side of a big yard. There we was kept until in the late fall, when I was sold to Louis Fortner, a rich planter with a big place near where Mason, Tenn. is." At first, she worked as a nurse, but the following summer, she was sent to the field. "I chopped cotton, plowed it and did everything any other slave done." This included training, or breaking, mules to accept the yoke of a plow. In one case, she harnessed a mule and "hitched him to a plow. We was doin' fine until he got scared at a snake hangin' down from a brush nearby, plunged ahead and dragged me over the plowhandles, breaking my right foot."

An advertisement for Nathan Bedford Forrest's slave market.

Betty Simmons was stolen from her owner, Leftwidge Carter, in Macedonia, Alabama. As she remembered in the 1930s, "These slave speculators puts the n----r man and me on the train and takes us to Memphis. And when we gets there they take us to the n----r traders' yard. We gets there at breakfast time and waits for the boat they calls the *Ohio* to get there....When it come, they was 258 n----rs out of them n----r yards in Memphis what gets on that boat." She ended up in New Orleans and was eventually sold to a Colonel Fortescue, who took her to Texas.

For many slaves, their only skill was picking cotton, which gave them few opportunities for meaningful employment after emancipation.

As Mary Herndon settled into her new life, Henry Davidson remained a slave to Thomas P. Davidson and a faithful member of Wesley Chapel, where he worked with the children of the church. It will be remembered that the Wesley Chapel African Mission had been formed in the basement of the church. In 1859, it outgrew the basement and relocated to a new building at the corner of Orleans Street and Washington Avenue. The first pastor was Joseph T.C. Collins, and the following year, the church was renamed Collins Chapel. It became one of the most important Black congregations in the city. Even though Collins Chapel was created specifically for African Americans, Henry Davidson remained at Wesley Chapel, which would become First Methodist Church in 1893.

In the late 1850s, C.F. Kholheim of Guntown, Mississippi, visited Forrest's slave yard with his father. While talking with Forrest in his office, Kholheim noticed a "big healthy fellow, resembling a Cherokee Indian more than anything else." His father asked Forrest if he was of African descent, and he replied that he was. Nevertheless, the slave had Indian roots. Forrest spoke to him in the Cherokee language, explaining, "I lived among the Cherokee long enough to master their language." He often

Henry Davidson was respected as one of the founders of First Methodist Church.

advertised having skilled workers available for sale. For example, he declared that his holdings included "two good blacksmiths" and "three good mechanics."

Being confined in these tightly packed markets often spread disease among the enslaved population. In April 1857, slaves died of consumption, whooping cough, measles, pneumonia, scarlet fever and typhoid fever. In addition to trafficking in mixed-race chattel, Forrest also participated in the international slave trade. In 1859, Forrest purchased thirty-seven Africans from the Congo who had been illegally smuggled into the United States. Thirty of them were sent to his Vicksburg, Mississippi market, and seven were offered in Memphis. He was not the least bit concerned about running afoul of the law because he allowed a *Memphis Daily Appeal* reporter to view the Africans and report on what he saw. "Persons feeling any interest to see the genuine native African can be gratified by calling at the Negro yard of our friend Forrest, on Adams Street....They are of short stature, very dark color, and generally a very slight in the make of the limbs, the ancle [*sic*] and wrist being very slender, and the hand small, with slender fingers, more like a woman's hand than a man's." The average cost of a slave in Forrest's market was $1,100, leading to an annual profit of $96,000. Elected to the city's board of aldermen in 1858, Forrest used his political power to benefit his human trafficking enterprise. In early 1859, a rival slave trader published the following advertisement in a local newspaper:

> *The Corporation charging more than I am able to pay for license, having been totally raised to about eight hundred dollars, including auction and negro license, brought forward by one of our city fathers in the same business as myself, so I have been told, but it is immaterial who was the originator of the outrageous tax, I for one, cannot pay it, therefore I wish to change my business, and will sell all the negroes on hand low for cash.*

Matilda was born in 1830 to a free Black family who were illegally being held as slaves. Abolitionist lawyers brought suit to free Matilda, her mother, her sister Mary Ellen and Mary Ellen's seven children. When he learned of the suit, a white man named Robert Logan seized the family and sold them to two Memphis slave traders named Collins and Woods. They were unconcerned with the family's questionable legal status, and neither was Nathan Bedford Forrest. He purchased them from Collins and Woods and made them available in his yard. Soon after they arrived in Memphis, Boss McGee was in the market for additional slaves. While inspecting the new

We Forrest & Maples Have this day sold, and do hereby convey to S. H. Dunscomb his heirs and assigns forever, for Eight hundred dollars, to us paid, for a slave named Mary aged about fifteen years of dark Complexion

We warrant the title to the said Slave to the said S.H. Dunscomb his heirs and assigns, against the lawful claim or claims of all persons; and We also warrant said Slave to be sound, healthy, sensible and Slave for life.

This 29th day of September, 1855

Forrest & Maples

In 1855, Forrest and Maples sold fifteen-year-old Mary for $800.

arrivals, he spied Matilda and Mary Ellen and immediately bought them. Matilda took over the cooking chores from Delia, and Mary Ellen was assigned to take care of Madam's sister, Mrs. Farrington. Tortured by the knowledge that she was free, Matilda's sad face and angry demeanor made the McGees uneasy; even Madam refrained from whipping her. Louis was drawn to this broken-hearted woman, and as time passed, the two fell in love. Boss had often promised Louis that when he decided to marry, he would give him a nice wedding. True to his word, Louis and Matilda were married in the McGees' parlor by the family's minister. "The wedding he gave us was indeed a pleasant one," Louis would later write. Happiness was fleeting for all slaves, as Louis learned when he overheard Old Master Jack remark, "It will ruin them, givin' wedins."

Madam's violent outbursts continued as Louis and Matilda settled into married life. She grew to hate Matilda, whose dignified manner frightened and enraged her. A year later, Matilda gave birth to twins, providing Madam with an instrument of revenge. Boss told Louis to help his wife in the kitchen so she would have time to nurse the babies. Madam had other plans. She increased his duties so he had no time to assist his wife in her work. According to Louis, a typical day for Matilda went like this:

> *In the morning she would nurse the babies, then hurry off to the kitchen to get breakfast while they were left in charge of a little girl. Again, at Noon she repeated her visit to the babies, after cooking the dinner, then in the evening, after supper, she would go to nurse them again. After supper was over, dishes all washed and kitchen in order, she would then go to the little ones for the night.*

The children began to wither away from lack of proper care. A doctor was called, and after examining Matilda, he stated that the babies were not getting enough nutrition because of their mother's "constant and excessive labors." Watching their children slowly die naturally had a profound effect on Louis and Matilda. At first, Matilda turned to faith. "God will help us, let us try and be patient," she told her husband. As time went on, however, both found themselves in the grip of despair. It was then that Madam chose to strike. One morning, she approached Matilda, vowing to give her a beating. "You shall not whip me," Matilda quietly declared. Madam flew into a rage, and Matilda fought back. In reply to Madam's screams, Boss arrived and grabbed Matilda by the throat. In the next room stood Louis, boiling with anger but shackled by fear and common sense. The violent moment soon passed, but Matilda had had enough. She grabbed her babies, packed their clothes and set out for downtown Memphis. All Louis could do was hand her a few coins he had collected from the tips of white people.

Railroads were used to transport slaves to be sold in Memphis.

Matilda marched straight to Forrest's slave market. As she sat beside the yard's back gate, it soon swung open, and Forrest passed through. "My God! Matilda, what are you doing here? You have changed so I would not have known you. Why have you come here?" Forrest asked. When she explained that she wanted to be sold because of the cruel treatment she received, Forrest replied, "I know these McGees, they are hard colts." He then called for the slave trader Collins, who expressed interest in buying her. While Collins was looking over Matilda, Boss arrived, vowing to never sell her. On their way back to the house, Boss turned to Matilda and said ominously, "When I'm through with you I guess you won't run away again." McGee placed her in the same wooden stocks that had once restrained her husband, and the couple took turns beating Matilda with a whip. As before, Louis stood nearby, "trembling from head to foot" for being unable to stop the torture of his wife. A few months later, their twin babies died. Not long after the burial of their children, Matilda walked into the smokehouse with Madam trailing behind, proclaiming, "I am tempted to take that knife from you, Matilda, and cut you in two. You…went all around the neighborhood and told the people that I killed your babies, and almost whipped you to death."

While Matilda and Louis were trying to recover from their unspeakable loss, the McGees' coachman Thomas was secretly trying to learn to read and write. Every evening, he snuck out of his quarters to meet an enslaved plasterer at his home who taught him enough to write simple sentences. After several months of practice, Thomas shared his newfound knowledge with Louis. Using chalk, Thomas wrote words on the side of the barn that Louis then tried to copy. Once, they forgot to wipe off the chalk marks, which were discovered by Old Master Jack. He confronted his son and said, "Edmund, you must watch those fellows, Louis and Thomas; if you don't, they will get spoilt." They convinced Boss that it wasn't them, but he remained suspicious. He told the Memphis postmaster to be on the lookout for any letters written to Thomas's mother in Virginia. Three letters were soon discovered and turned over to McGee. The next morning, Boss called for Thomas to come and be whipped. Louis heard the call and snuck around the barn so he could hear. "Where did you learn to write and when did you learn?" Refusing to answer, Thomas was severely beaten. A few weeks later, he forged a pass in McGee's name and ran away. The forged document gave Thomas permission to hire himself out to any employer who would accept him and for as long as needed. Thomas boarded a steamboat and confidently presented his credential to the pilot. Hired on the spot, Thomas made good his escape from the McGees and Memphis. Landing at New Orleans, he boarded a ship bound for Boston and was soon long gone from the slave South. Boss tried to retrieve him, but to no avail. Six months later,

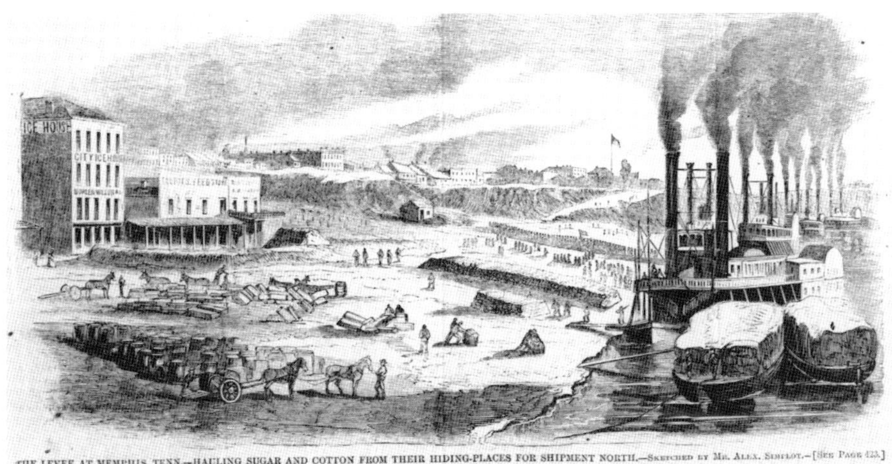

The Memphis wharf where Thomas Bland successfully escaped from the McGee family.

Louis picked up the mail from the post office, including a letter from Canada. When Boss finished the letter, he must have been in a boiling rage, for it was correspondence from Thomas, telling him that he was now free in Canada. McGee's nephew later confirmed this when he reported seeing Thomas in Niagara Falls. Boss hurried to upstate New York with a pair of handcuffs in hopes of capturing his runaway, but Thomas was never found.

The fact that skilled slaves knew how to read and write and felt comfortable, even free, to pass this information along suggests the unique place skilled slaves, also known as mechanics, occupied within the slave system. They were sometimes given the opportunity to hire themselves out to local businesses where they were paid wages and, like the plasterer who taught Thomas how to read, live in their own homes. Usually, the slave would be required to share his wages with his owner and report on his activities and expenses. According to historian Midori Takagi, "It became common for urban slaves to live with their own families in separate communities." This is why it was so easy for Thomas to gain employment on a steamboat. Nearly all the building and manufacturing trades in Memphis employed slaves. Adam Lock worked as a plasterer, and Albert Harris was a shoemaker owned by J.B. Griffin and Company. Before he was sold to W. Fitzgerald of Senatobia, Mississippi, Bill Trezevant had been employed as a waiter at the Worsham House and the Commercial Hotel. Working for hotels and restaurants was one of the most common forms of urban slave labor. Noted writer and landscape architect Frederick Law Olmsted traveled through the South in the 1850s and recorded his observations in the book *The Cotton Kingdom: A Traveller's Observations on Cotton and Slavery in the American Slave States, 1853–1861*. In Memphis, he stayed at the Commercial Hotel, where he was served by slave waiters in the restaurant. The best accommodation in Memphis was the Gayoso House, which owned many slaves, including Alfred, Foster, George, Henry and Lewis.

In 1851, the Methodist Conference appointed Daniel H. Jones as the slave pastor of First Methodist Church's Black congregation. That same year, Samuel P. Walker purchased Jack Harris Walker and brought him to the city. In an 1866 interview, Walker stated that he "always hired my own time since I have been in Memphis, some fifteen years," Slaves were also employed by the Memphis and Ohio Railroad. David was a fifty-year-old who was hired out by his owner, M.C. Cayce, as a carpenter.

Other skilled slaves included Dan Thomas, who was owned by a whiskey manufacturer and saloon operator. Dan helped make whiskey and, when he was older, tended bar and collected the bills owed the company. "I would go out to collect bills from Marster's customers and it took me about a week to get all 'round. I wasn't allowed to take money, but had to get their checks," remembered Thomas. Ben was a banjo player owned by Bolton, Dickens and Co. and sold to Hawkins on December 19, 1856. Although many whites

MEMPHIS, TENN., August 19 1859

Received of S B Williamson

Thirteen hundred Dollars

in full, for the Purchase Money of a Negro man

named Foster aged about

nineteen years

said Negro we warrant sound and healthy in body and mind, and Slave for life.

We warrant also the title to the same goods, and perfect against all claims whatever.

Given under our hand the day and date above written.

Hill Ware [illegible]

An 1859 receipt for the purchase of nineteen-year-old Foster for $1,300.

profited from slaves hiring themselves out, others denounced the practice. In a letter to the *Memphis Daily Eagle*, a white citizen declared that "to permit a Negro to hire his own time sends a slave to ruin as property, debauches a slave, and makes him a strolling agent of discontent, disorder, and immorality among our slave population."

He was right about one thing: there was a streak of "immorality" in the slave population. There were many reasons for this. Slaves were as susceptible to temptation as any human and had the added reason of wanting to resist their condition. For example, Jack committed burglary and attempted murder in 1832. Albert was arrested for fighting, Moses was thrown in jail for driving his wagon on the pavement and Reed was arrested for "working without a pass." Pat liked to drive his wagon faster than the law allowed and sometimes slept in it, while Robert was arrested for visiting a saloon. In May 1859, four slaves working in the kitchen of the Redford House were busy gambling when police stormed the building. Quickly arrested, they were each sentenced to receive thirty-nine lashes from a whip. Lawson was arrested when he concealed a runaway slave named Mandy, and Ned was picked up for having a forged pass. Dave liked to steal, as did Edmond, who was arrested for "larceny of chickens." Frank, George, Jacob and many others enjoyed drinking to excess and often found themselves in the calaboose.

While some slaves were behind bars, others became entangled in the court system. The Shelby County Chancery Court ordered the clerk and master to sell Ann at auction to settle the case of Elizabeth, Mary and William Braswell v. Benjamin Askew and D.M. Sanderlin, and Lucinda was deeded by M.G. Ward to B.M. Estes in order to pay his debts. A five-year-old boy named Baner was auctioned off in pursuance of a chancery court decree in regard to the suit of Lucy W. Stark, administratrix of Henry C. Stark, deceased, and others, v. Margaret Stark, Louisiana Farabee and others, creditors of Henry C. Stark, deceased. Betty was sold by the Shelby County sheriff on order of the circuit court judge in favor of R.E. Orne v. John Coleman and R.T.G. Hart. Not all court actions resulted in the

SLAVE DEALERS.

BOLTON, DICKENS & Co. Front Row south of Union
Delap & Witherspoon, 59 Adams
HILL, BYRD, & SON, 56 Adams
Nevill & Cunningham, 69 Adams
Noel, G. N. 39 Monroe
FORREST & MAPLES, 87 Adams

List of slave traders in Memphis in 1855.

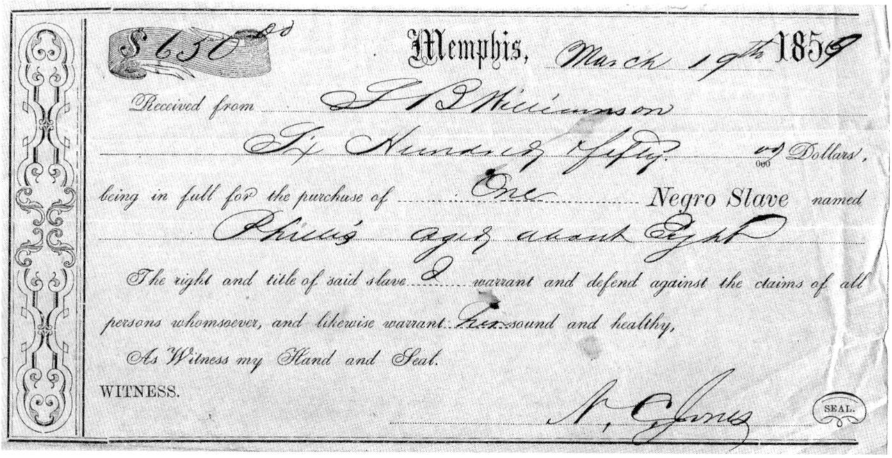

$650 00/100 Memphis, March 19th 1859

Received from S. B. Williamson

Six Hundred Fifty 00/100 Dollars,

being in full for the purchase of One Negro Slave named

Phillis aged about Eight

The right and title of said slave I warrant and defend against the claims of all persons whomsoever, and likewise warrant her sound and healthy,

As Witness my Hand and Seal.

WITNESS.

N. C. Jones (SEAL.)

One of the most horrible aspects of slavery was the buying and selling of children. Here is an 1859 receipt for the purchase of an eight-year-old child named Phillis.

sale of slaves. In many cases, they led to freedom. When Caesar A. Jones died in 1849, David Jones was emancipated. Twenty-six-year-old Beck, twenty-one-year-old Rachel, a one-year-old child named Aleck, five-year-old Clementine, two-year-old James and a four-year-old mulatto named Clarissa were given their freedom in 1850, while Ned was set free in 1853. David Jones successfully petitioned the court to stay in Memphis, where he eked out a living doing odd jobs.

A year after Ned was emancipated, Congress passed the Kansas-Nebraska Act, which voided the Missouri Compromise and adopted Illinois senator Stephen Douglas's doctrine of popular sovereignty, which allowed the white citizens of each territory to decide on their own whether they wanted slavery or not. Then in 1857, the United States Supreme Court handed down its decision in *Dred Scott v. Sandford*. The case was brought by a Missouri slave named Dred Scott, who argued that when his owner took him to a free state, he immediately became a free man. In its decision, the court declared that Scott—and all Americans of African descent, whether slave or free—had no constitutional rights and therefore could not sue in any court. The ruling also stated that Congress could not prevent slave owners from taking and holding their property in any part of the United States. When the Kansas-Nebraska Act was passed and the *Dred Scott* decision was handed down, white northerners believed that the "slave power" controlling the South was determined to spread slavery to every corner of the nation. At the same time, white southerners believed that abolitionists and the newly formed Republican Party were equally determined to destroy slavery and their way of life. This deepening sectional conflict soon became irrepressible.

As the lives of Henry Davidson, Louis and Matilda Hughes, Delia, Ned, Thomas and Daniel H. Jones attest, slavery was woven into every sphere of Memphis life. It appeared to be so deeply entrenched that nothing could dislodge it. However, as 1859 came to an end, the looming presidential election offered a grain of hope to the enslaved of Memphis and the South while angering those who kept them in chains.

Chapter 4

"WE'RE GOIN' TO BE FREE"

1860–1865

In 1860, Mary Herndon was still chopping cotton on the Fortner Farm, and Louis and Matilda Hughes continued to live under the wrath of Boss and Madam. The sectional crisis between the free labor North and slave South reached a boiling point when the Republican Party chose the lanky former rail-splitter and congressman Abraham Lincoln as its presidential nominee. The party and its standard-bearer were unalterably opposed to slavery and its spread into new territories. This put Lincoln on a collision course with the white South, which was determined to preserve slavery and expand its reach. Edmund McGee, Louis Fortner and many other slave owners opposed Lincoln and vowed drastic action if he was elected. When that came to pass in November, Herndon overheard Fortner say, "There goin' to be war." The McGees had a similar reaction when they read of Lincoln's election in the newspapers. "The very idea of electing an old rail splitter to the presidency of the United States," sputtered Boss. "Well…he'll never take his seat."

Meanwhile, slaves continued to flee whenever they got the chance. Bob ran away from Dr. Merrill Harrison, while Isaac left the home of Dr. R. Olman. A "dark mulatto, with a full bushy head of hair and a large unshaven beard, above the medium height, intelligent, can read and write, and is very pompous in his language and actions, and about thirty years of age," by the name of Henry, ran away from J.M.M. Cornelius of the rural Shelby County hamlet of Germantown. Cat was able to secure five dollars before running away from S. Richards, and Harrison had a pocketbook and knife with him when he was caught. At the same time, other slaves engaged

State of So Carolina } Recd from Robert McCorcle
Lancaster District } husband of the now Mary
McCorcle daughter of Elijah Crockett deceased his receipt
in full of their dividend of both real and personal Estate
of the said Elijah Crocket and also the said Robert McCorcle's
receipt for whatever may appear to be my daughter Mary
McCorcle's dividend of my estate at my death being
in full satisfaction of a negro girl named Marriah
a bout ten years old which Negro girl I now give and deliver
unto the said Robert ~~McCorcle~~ for to remain as the property
of them the said Robert McCorcle and Mary his wife for
and during the natural life time of her the said Mary
McCorcle and at the death of her the said Mary McCorcle
the said Negro Marriah and her issue (if any) to remain
in one Common Stock unto the youngest legitimate of
the said Mary McCorcle shall arrive of at the age of
twenty One years or be married at which time the said
Negro Marriah and her issue shall be divided share
and share alike equally between the legal issue of the said
Mary McCorkle which said negro Marriah I do forever
Warrant and defend unto the said Mary McCorcle and her
issue against myself my heirs and Exrs & Administrators
and against the just and legal claim or claims of any
person or persons whomsoever. In witness whereof
I have hereunto set my hand and seal this 20th day of October
1815 Signed sealed and acknowledged
in the presence of } Mary her X mark Crocket
Robert Crockett
Andw Crockett

Probate document leaving a slave named Marriah to Mary McCorkle.

in criminality. Jack, Marcus, Mary, Philis, Robert and Spence were found drunk on the streets of Memphis. Ebb was knifed to death, while James engaged in fighting, Mingo committed larceny, and Kemp was arrested for attempted rape. The most sensational crime occurred in 1860, when a group of slaves owned by Clayton Rogers murdered their overseer, James Powers.

Under Article VII of the Constitution, states joined the Union by electing a popular convention to ratify the decision. Many in the South were convinced that this procedure also allowed states to leave the Union. South Carolina was the first to act. On December 17, 1860, the state convention declared, "The Union now subsisting between South Carolina and the other States under the name of the United States of America is hereby dissolved." Mississippi, Florida, Alabama, Georgia, Louisiana and Texas held their own conventions, and each voted to leave the Union. At first, Tennessee followed this example. In February 1861, the general assembly scheduled a statewide referendum so voters could decide whether or not a secession convention should be held. Just before the election, a large procession gathered at the Exchange Building and marched through the streets of Memphis. According to a reporter from the *Memphis Daily Appeal*, the parade included hundreds carrying torches while wagons, horses and floats passed between them. On one float was an effigy of the anti-secession Tennessee senator Andrew Johnson with a banner that exclaimed, "I Have No Respect for a Traitor!" Other signs declared, "Our Fathers Fought for Freedom from One Tyrant, We Fight for Freedom from Millions of Tyrants" and "Negro Slavery, It Must and Shall Be Preserved. We Make No More Compromises." White voters in Memphis voted overwhelmingly for a secession convention, but a majority of the state's voters rejected the measure.

On March 4, 1861, the day Abraham Lincoln was inaugurated the sixteenth president of the United States, Edmund McGee met in his home with several like-minded slave owners to discuss what course to take. By this time, seven states had seceded from the Union and formed a separate nation called the Confederate States of America. According to Louis Hughes, the men were "wild with excitement," vowing to "whip the Yankees, five or six to one." Five weeks later, Confederate artillery bombarded Fort Sumter in Charleston Harbor, beginning the war so many Memphians had hoped for. City government allocated $59,000 for Memphis's defense; established an armory filled with ammunition, cannon and rifles; and erected a wall of cotton bales on the riverfront to protect Memphis from attack. One day, Louis drove Boss into town so he could shop at a dry goods store. When he returned to the wagon, he excitedly told Louis, "What do you think? Old Abraham Lincoln has called for four hundred thousand men to come to Washington immediately. Well, let them come; we will make breakfast of them. I can whip a half dozen Yankees with my pocketknife." In Memphis, militia units were formed, including one joined by McGee's nephew Edward Dandridge. Mary Herndon visited Memphis during this time and witnessed these nascent soldiers drilling and practicing marksmanship. In Nashville, Governor Isham Harris refused to send troops to stop the rebellion and called the general assembly into special session. They wasted little time in declaring Tennessee's independence and creating a fifty-five-thousand-man army. Then, on June 8, a second referendum was held, and the citizens of Tennessee voted to leave the United States. Three weeks later, Tennessee joined the Confederate States of America. Although an ardent secessionist, Boss was unwilling to risk his life for the cause. Instead, he hired a substitute to fight in his place. He still wanted to kill a Yankee or two, so he bought a pistol and practiced every afternoon. Louis accompanied Boss on these "field exercises," and while he set the targets and made the bullets, he thought to himself that McGee was "very ludicrous" to play at war while refusing to fight.

Two months after Tennessee joined a nation committed to preserving slavery, the United States Congress took its first step toward destroying that institution. On August 6, 1861, it passed the Confiscation Act, which granted Union forces the authority to seize property and slaves being used for rebellion against the United States. Lincoln opposed the law for fear the remaining slave states would use it as an excuse to abandon the United States. When Union generals attempted to implement the law, Lincoln repudiated their actions, and the War Department ordered officers not to interfere with slavery. However, the law laid a foundation for later actions, and when news reached them, it gave the enslaved hope that their bondage was nearing its end. Louis often heard slaves whispering to themselves, "We will be free." "They would laugh and chat about freedom in their cabins; and many a little rhyme about it originated among them and was softly sung over their work." One day, Old Master Jack's wife overheard their cook Kitty singing, "There'll be no more talk about Monday, by and by, but every day will be Sunday, by and by." Old Mrs. McGee snapped, "Don't think you are going to be free; you darkies were made by God and ordained to wait upon us." As Old Lady McGee's outburst suggests, slavery continued with little interruption. Young and Weld's sold a "no. 1 hand" for $1,000 and an eighteen-year-old "efficient house servant" for $250. Alice ran away from J.W. Crisp and Company; I.T. Cartwright advertised to hire "good cooks, dining room and house servants"; John Marshall was brought to Memphis; and Elick was owned by Shelby County, where he worked in the courthouse. Nathan Bedford Forrest closed his slave market and joined the Confederate army, but A.S. Levy and Company and Byrd Hill continued to sell slaves. On May 26, 1861, F.W. Royester and Co. advertised that it had available "a lot

Slaves helped construct Fort Pillow for both the Confederate and Union armies.

of No. 1 Virginia raised Negroes, among them good cooks and seamstresses. Also, a boy, 16 years of age, who is a good dining room servant. They are not sold for any fault."

The Confederate army routinely hired slaves to work on fortifications. For example, the Confederate provost marshal in Memphis declared that "two hundred Negroes are urgently wanted to go to Fort Pillow," which was located sixty miles north of the city on the Mississippi River. In January 1862, T.W. Potter wanted to hire "a good cook, washer, and ironer; a girl about thirteen and a boy fifteen years of age." A few months later, sixty-year-old Jane Nunn was brought to Memphis. The following month, the Confederate assistant quartermaster, Captain N.L. Lawrence, hired one hundred slaves at forty dollars per month to "crew government transports between Memphis and Columbus, Kentucky." David Jones, who had been freed in 1850 when his owner, Caesar Jones, died, became a body servant to a Confederate officer serving under General Nathan Bedford Forrest. Edmund Turley followed his owner, Thomas B. Turley, into the Confederate army. When his owner was captured, Edmund served under Forrest's command until the end of the war. In 1868, the former slave trader was interviewed by a congressional committee investigating "the condition of affairs in the late insurrectionary states." In his testimony, he explained:

> *When I entered the army, I took forty-seven Negroes into the army with me, and forty-five of them were surrendered with me. I said to them at the start: "This fight is against slavery; if we lose it, you will be made free; if we whip in the fight, and if you stay with me and be good boys, I will set you free. In either case you will be free." Those boys stayed with me, drove my teams, and better confederates did not live.*

Perhaps he had no choice, but the available records do not tell us why a free person of color like David Jones would join the Confederate army as little more than a slave.

On April 6, 1862, Confederate forces commanded by Albert Sidney Johnston broke the lines of General U.S. Grant near Shiloh Church, one hundred miles east of Memphis. When word reached Memphis, Edmund McGee was beside himself with joy. "Lou, Lou, come," he yelled. "We have a great victory." Louis had no reason to celebrate, but he did have to obey Boss's order to prepare food for the victorious soldiers. He and Matilda spent the day making biscuits, ham, hoecakes, tongue and other foodstuffs, which were loaded into a large basket that normally hauled cotton. The basket was then placed in a wagon, and Boss headed toward the Rebel lines. As he traveled toward Shiloh, McGee had no way of knowing that Union and Confederate forces had resumed the battle. Grant had been reinforced during the night and, with his superior force, pushed the Confederates back

When word of the Union victory at Shiloh reached Memphis, slaves secretly rejoiced, while many whites fled the city.

to nearby Corinth, Mississippi. McGee caught up with the retreating Rebels, where he discovered his nephew Edward Dandridge had been killed in the battle. He dashed off a telegram to his wife and prepared to have the body shipped to Memphis. Louis was working in the dining room when a messenger approached the house with a telegram for Mrs. McGee, who read it and sorrowfully passed it to her sister, Mrs. Charles Dandridge. Crushed by the news that her son was dead, Mrs. Dandridge wept inconsolably. The body arrived the following day, and Louis assisted in preparing it for burial. They washed and dressed the body and painted the face because it was blackened from lying exposed on the battlefield. Louis watched as Edward's parents, aunts and uncles descended the staircase and entered the parlor. Calmly, Mrs. Dandridge approached the casket, turned to Boss and said, "Cousin Eddie, how brave he was! He died for his country." Slavery may have forced Louis to stand silently by, but it could not control his mind. "Poor, sorrowing, misguided woman," Louis thought to himself. "It was not for his country he died, but for the perpetuation of the cruel, the infamous system of human slavery." In the end, it came down to this. One group of Southerners saw the Civil War as a noble conflict to win independence for an oppressed minority, while another group, who weren't even really considered Southerners or Americans, knew the war was being fought by the Confederacy to keep them in chains. However, Louis and Matilda Hughes, Mary Herndon and many others looked for opportunities to break their shackles.

The Union victory at Shiloh left west Tennessee and Memphis exposed to the Union army. Fearing the loss of their slaves, the McGee family decided to flee the Bluff City. Soon after they arrived safely at Old Master Jack's place in Panola County, Boss took Louis to his farm in Bolivar County, Mississippi, where he was put in charge of the dining room. While Louis performed his duties and Boss nervously kept watch for Federal activity, a Union steamer chugged down the river and was captured near the McGee farm by Confederate soldiers. Knowing more Union vessels would move into the area, Boss ordered Louis to keep a close watch on the river. One morning, he yelled for Boss when he spied a Union gunboat gliding toward the landing. Mounting his horse, McGee galloped right into a squad of Union soldiers, who promptly arrested him. He and a few other white plantation owners were sent under guard to the jail in Helena, Arkansas.

Back in Memphis, the city was on edge. In late May, all Confederate troops left the city, leaving behind a handful of soldiers guarding the roads into Memphis and a small fleet of Rebel gunboats patrolling the Mississippi River. Slave traders paid little heed. On June 3, 1862, the firm of Passmore,

Union forces occupied Memphis in June 1862, which provided opportunities for slaves to escape their bondage.

Lide and Marshall auctioned slaves at its office located at the corner of Court and Main Streets. Three days later, white Memphians watched in horror as a Union flotilla approached the Confederate fleet and promptly destroyed it. Left with no more defenses, Memphis surrendered to the Union army. Among the witnesses to that day was Cynthia Townsend, who had been a slave in Memphis for eighteen years before purchasing her freedom a few days before the battle. Included in the Confederate fleet was the paddle-wheel steamer *Victoria*. On board the vessel was a twenty-three-year-old slave named Robert Church, who was also the son of the captain, Charles Church. Robert was spared the worst aspects of slavery; his father treated him well and once told him, "Don't let anyone call you n----r." Nevertheless, Robert longed to be free. As the naval battle raged, Robert jumped into the river and swam to shore. It did not matter that he was cold and wet; he was free for the first time in his life.

What did Federal occupation mean for slavery? No doubt that weighed on the minds of most Memphians, Black and white. As we have seen, Congress passed the Confiscation Act, which allowed for the seizure of slaves to deny the Rebels their labor. President Lincoln, however, ordered slavery to be left alone. Slaves were not concerned with the president's political problems; they took matters into their own hands. Like Robert Church, they made their way to the Union lines in search of liberty. David, a forty-year-old plasterer, ran away from M.H. Baldwin on June 15. Many acted as unofficial spies,

In June 1862, Robert Church Sr. jumped into the Mississippi River at Memphis to escape slavery.

reporting on Confederate movements in the area. For example, on June 18, former slaves informed Union general Lew Wallace that a Rebel force was camped in the village of Germantown, thirteen miles from Memphis. As a result of their information, Federal troops routed the Confederates from their position, which strengthened the Union occupation. On the same day, Major General William T. Sherman, commanding the Army of the Tennessee, issued Order No. 43, which declared:

> *The commanding general must call attention to the duties of officers and men toward the slaves. The well-settled policy of the whole army now is to have nothing to do with the Negro. "Exclude them from camp" is General Halleck's reiterated order. We cannot have our trains encumbered by them, nor can we afford to feed them, and it is deceiving the poor fellow to allow him to start and have him forcibly driven away afterward.... The laws of Congress command that we do not surrender back to the master a fugitive slave....Also the laws of war make the property of the enemy liable to confiscation if used for warlike purposes....In such cases*

> *the commanding officer would rightfully appropriate his labor through the quartermaster and let the title to freedom be tried as soon as a possible civil tribunal can be reached.*

Headquartered in Memphis, the commander of the West Tennessee District, Major General U.S. Grant, reported on July 8 that he had gathered a group of former slaves, referred to as contrabands, to work on fortifying the south end of the city. Nine days later, Congress passed the second Confiscation Act. The legislation declared that all slaves belonging to civilian and military officials were now free. In response to the second Confiscation Act, the Union army changed its position on taking care of former slaves. In Order No. 60, Sherman, who succeeded Grant as West Tennessee District commander, clarified how slaves were to be treated: "While negroes are employed on public works, fortifications, driving teams, and such public work, they will be subsisted by the officer in charge." Sherman also made provision for each contraband to receive a one-pound ration of chewing tobacco per month, as well as shirts, pants and shoes. Soon there were more contrabands than Union forces could handle. In December 1862, Grant appointed Presbyterian minister and infantry chaplain John Eaton as general superintendent of contrabands. He established a contraband camp near Memphis on a river bluff. Eaton did his best, but there were no funds provided for food and shelter, which resulted in the death of 1,200 contrabands during the winter of 1862–63. In early 1863, Eaton established a camp on President's Island. A much safer location than the other camps, it soon became the largest contraband facility in West Tennessee. At President's Island, the former slaves lived in rough log cabins, and a crude hospital provided some medical care and the opportunity for a few to work as nurses. Other contrabands cut wood for steamboats or worked for Union military authorities. Conditions were often terrible, but few were willing to exchange discomfort for slavery.

In late August, Sherman received a letter from a West Point classmate named Thomas Hunton, who owned a plantation in Panola County, Mississippi, not too far from the McGee plantation. Hunton asked his old friend to search for and return to him a group of runaway slaves. In his reply, Sherman sharply told him, "We are enemies, still private friends. In the one capacity I will do you all the harm I can." He went on to state that he found "no negroes registered as belong to Hunton, some in the name of McGhee [more likely Edmund McGee or some of his kin]." Sherman continued to tell Hunton, "I will moreover see that they are one and all told what is true of all—Boys, if you want to go to your master, go—you are free to choose. You must now think for yourselves; your master has seceded from his parent government and you have seceded from him." On September 3, 1862, Sherman wrote his brother John, a United States senator from Ohio, explaining how he was dealing with the slave question:

> *Now I have my orders appropriated the labor of Negroes as far as will benefit the army. To injure our enemy universal emancipation with the machinery to carry into effect would of course be effectual, but by no means conclusive. Not one n----r in ten wants to run off—there are 25,000 in 20 miles of Memphis—all could escape & would receive protection here, but we have only about 2,000 of whom full one half are hanging about camps as officers' servants.*

Six weeks after Sherman's letter, he ordered his provost marshal to take control of the civilian and military police and treat all slaves as freedmen. Sherman's order was quickly challenged when the next Shelby County Grand Jury met. Criminal court judge John T. Swayne required grand jurors to continue to indict anyone who violated state and local slave codes. Angry at Swayne's impertinence, Sherman declared that the army would not allow any convictions to stand because "no law of Tennessee in conflict with the Law of the United States, for the latter is the Law and if any Lawyer or Judge thinks different, the quicker he gets out of the United States, the safer his neck will be."

No doubt Judge Swayne wanted to keep his neck safe, so he modified his position by telling the next grand jury that it had no power to defy the Union army. A few slave owners began to realize they, too, could no longer resist

In July 1862, Union major general U.S. Grant appropriated the labor of former slaves to fortify the south end of the city.

the onward march of freedom. Since growing to manhood, Henry Davidson continued to serve both his owner, Thomas P. Davidson, and Wesley Chapel. As the Union occupation intensified, Henry was given his freedom, as were James E. Donahue and Lucy Hunt. However, others remained firmly in bondage. Mary Herndon recalled that "one night, Massa' come home from Memphis. He says, 'they tell me all the n----rs are goin' to be set free. If I believed it, I'd take a gun and kill every damn one of them rather than see them fall into the hands of the Yankees.'" After they all went to bed, someone set fire to the Fortners' barn, which contained hundreds of bales of cotton. Two days later, a Union soldier passed through and told all of Fortner's slaves that they were free. Herndon didn't know how to act on this news, but it did alter how she saw herself. Soon after, Mrs. Fortner gave Herndon an order she didn't want to obey. When she replied that she was free, Fortner screamed, "You are not free. You get that hoe and go to the field." "I sassed her again and she up with a hoe and hit me on the head." Mary Herndon carried the deep scar from that wound for the rest of her life.

A few days before Christmas, Boss and the other Confederate prisoners proposed to the Union commander at Helena a trade. In exchange for their freedom, they would arrange for the release of the crew of the captured Federal steamer. A messenger was dispatched to Bolivar with the terms, but on his way back to Helena, he joined a party and became stinking drunk. Unable to finish his mission, Louis was ordered to complete the journey. He carried the documents to Fryer's Point, where an acquaintance delivered them to Helena. From there, he traveled to the Panola plantation to tell Madam of Boss's capture. He arrived on Christmas Eve to a household filled with despair. Three days later, he was on his way back to Fryer's Point with a packet of letters for Boss. From there, he was to go back to the Bolivar Farm, but instead he doubled back to Old Master Jack's to tell Matilda he was running away. After several miles of climbing wooded hills and passing through dirty swamps, he briefly rested. Surrounded by a dark mist that obscured his vision, Louis suddenly heard a voice cry out, "Halt! Advance and give the countersign." When he didn't answer, the voice demanded he "come right up here or I'll blow you to eternity." Louis stepped forward and found himself facing the bore of a Confederate musket. As he shook with fear, Louis told the Rebel soldier that he was on an errand for his owner and became lost. He was then taken to the Confederate camp, where he was accused of being a Union spy. Fortunately, he was recognized by a Confederate officer, who fetched Old Master Jack to the camp. The Confederate captain informed Old Master Jack they planned to execute

Louis for being a spy. "I know Edmund would not have him hung. He is too valuable. No, no!" Unable to kill Louis, the Rebels instead whipped him mercilessly and marched him to the Panola jail. They stopped by Old Master Jack's, where Matilda was allowed to see her husband. Distraught and fearing for his life, Matilda was slightly comforted by a soldier who told her, "Don't cry, aunty, we are not going to hang him—we will only put him in jail." Soon after leaving the McGee place, they learned the jail had been destroyed by Union raiders. Left with no other alternative, the Confederates took Louis back to Old Master Jack's, where he was reunited with his wife.

On New Year's Day 1863, President Lincoln's Emancipation Proclamation went in to effect and expanded the Second Confiscation Act to include "all persons held as slaves within any State or designated part of a State, the people whereof shall then be in rebellion against the United States, shall be then, thenceforward, and forever free." Lincoln went on to state that the federal government "will recognize and maintain the freedom of said persons." Finally, the president also authorized that "such persons of suitable condition, will be received into the armed service of the United States to garrison forts, positions, stations, and other places, and to man vessels of all sorts in said service." The Emancipation Proclamation not only clarified federal policy toward former slaves and allowed them to serve in the military, but it also transformed the goal of the war from maintaining the union of states into a conflict dedicated to eradicating slavery. Being able to serve in the military emboldened many slaves to flee their condition. Henry Gamble Burford fled his owners' Mississippi plantation to join the Union army, where he served as a private in the Third Colored Artillery stationed in Memphis. Horace Mayweathers, who washed dishes in his owners' boardinghouse, also joined the Union army and served for the rest of the war. In 1863, Rastus Jones joined a group of runaways from DeSoto County, Mississippi, as they made their way to Memphis. Joining the Union army, Jones was attached to Grant's command as a cook. He was with Grant when Vicksburg was captured and then moved east with forces assigned to Sherman's invasion of Georgia. Captured near Marietta, Georgia, in the summer of 1864, Jones was thrown into a Confederate prison until the war ended.

While Rastus Jones and Horace Mayweathers were serving the Union cause, other former slaves in Memphis organized themselves politically. On January 1, 1864, a large number of Black Memphians gathered at Middle Baptist Church on Second Street to commemorate the first anniversary of the Emancipation Proclamation and pass a resolution in support of the war effort. Reverend David Randolph of Middle Baptist was appointed

The existence of Union soldiers in Memphis and the surrounding territory gave hope to slaves that they soon would be free.

chair, while Horatio N. Rankin, a teacher with the Western Freedman's Aid Commission, was appointed secretary. James Hicks, George W. Preston and Union sergeants Warren Brown and Louis Murray were selected vice presidents, and Sergeant John C. Scurlock was named assistant to the secretary. Several resolutions were introduced, and many were adopted. The final resolution praised Union soldiers and called on African American men to join the military, "where he can successfully perform his duty to his God, his country, and his fellow-men." The document went on to boldly declare, "As this is our country, and we are citizens of the United States…therefore, we are willing to defend them with life and limb; and after protecting them with our guns, we humbly pray God that there may be generosity enough left to protect us in our native land." We should pause a moment over the statement "we are citizens of the United States." Blacks, whether free or slave, had rarely made such a declaration in so public a forum. By claiming citizenship and expressing their willingness to fight for that status, Black Memphians crossed over a psychological barrier that had helped keep them in bondage for decades.

All across the South, slaves such as Rastus Jones were crippling the Confederate war effort by fleeing to the Union lines or, like Mary Herndon, resisting their white owners however they could. Slaves were destroying the institution from within as the Union army, Congress and President Lincoln attacked it from without. However, permanently eradicating the institution was very much in doubt. Lincoln knew that his Emancipation Proclamation might not pass constitutional muster once the rebellion was over. It had been emphasized that emancipation and confiscation were war measures needed to achieve victory over a civil rebellion. Once that ended, would there be no legal protections for the former slaves? In February 1864, the Senate Judiciary Committee answered this question by proposing a Thirteenth Amendment to the Constitution that would abolish slavery within the United States. On April 8, the full Senate passed the amendment by a vote of thirty-eight yeas to six nays. Two months later, pro-amendment members of the House of Representatives were unable to secure a two-thirds majority, and the measure was defeated. When Republicans gathered that same month, June 1864, to nominate the president for a second term, they drafted a platform that stated, "We are in favor, furthermore, of such an amendment to the Constitution, to be made by the people in conformity with its provisions, as shall terminate and forever prohibit the existence of Slavery within the limits of the jurisdiction of the United States."

Back in Panola County, Louis Hughes was again making plans to escape the McGees. He joined forces with Alfred Dandridge, who as a teamster was very familiar with the roads to Memphis. One dark evening, Louis and Alfred—along with Matilda, Dandridge's wife, and another slave named Matt—slipped away and headed for the Bluff City. Using the stars as a guide, Alfred led them through briar patches, dense woods and swamps. "We stumbled on, however, as best we could, each fearful, yet silently praying for guidance and help," Louis remembered. The baying of hounds drove them into a swampy area, where Alfred oiled their feet with a mixture of turpentine and onions. Each ran in a different direction as the hounds grew closer. Williams "the n----r-catcher" and fourteen vicious dogs caught up to Louis just as he was climbing a persimmon tree. When he climbed down, the hounds snapped at his clothes and bit his flesh. The others were quickly rounded up, and they stopped at a nearby farm before heading back to Old Master Jack's. "You n----rs going to the Yankees? You all ought to be killed," said the owner of the farm. When they returned, Old Lady McGee, Master Jack's wife, screamed at Matilda, "I thought you were a Christian. You'll never see your God." She then had all of the escapees whipped—in a Christian way, of course. Shortly after their failed escape attempt, Louis and Matilda were sent to Atlanta to keep them from the clutches of the Union army. While traveling through Alabama, they found themselves reunited with Edmund McGee, whom they had not seen since his capture in 1862. Boss had been set free from the Helena jail but, instead of returning to his wife and family, moved to the Tombigbee River, where he operated a salt manufacturing operation for the Confederate government. Louis and Matilda stayed with Boss until he unexpectedly died on New Year's Day 1865. Louis and Matilda were hired out to work at the salt works until Union troops forced them to return to Old Master Jack's.

While Louis and Matilda were making their way back to Panola County, many former slaves remained stuck in the contraband camp on President's Island. Most of them couldn't leave because they were former field hands who had no skills to employ in an urban setting. A school was established there by the Western Freedmen's Aid Commission, but it had few resources despite the skill of a teacher named Horatio Rankin. This situation was replicated in contraband camps across the South. As we have seen, many Union officers had tried to improve the situation, with little success. In response to this, Congress passed "An Act to Establish a Bureau for the Relief of Freedmen and Refugees" on March 3, 1865, to provide food, shelter and educational opportunities for displaced persons in the South, especially former slaves. In June 1865, the Memphis Sub-District of the Freedmen's Bureau rented a building on Beale Street for a school, and the following month, Davis Tillson was named superintendent. Tillson and his successors—A.T. Reeve, Benjamin Runkle and Fred S. Palmer—supervised the work of field agents who reported on the conditions of former slaves, negotiated labor contracts and distributed relief. A bank was established for their use, a special court heard their cases and the subdistrict office certified their marriages.

The winter cold hung over Panola County as Louis drifted off to sleep. Later, the sound of heavy wagons woke him from his slumber. Jumping out of bed, he walked outside and saw wagons pulling heavy artillery. The next morning, he was ordered to take a package to James McGee, who was at a Confederate camp near Como, Mississippi. Riding out of the big gate onto the main road, he was accosted by a Union officer who stole his horse and package. Left with the officer's mount, he slowly rode back to the house, but when he arrived, the yard was full of Union soldiers. Louis ran into the house to tell Madam the Yankees were there and had stolen his horse. When he heard the news, Old Master Jack bravely called for a "mush poultice" and took to his bed. Kitty, Louis, Matilda, Alfred and the other slaves had a far different reaction. "Ah, we're goin' to be free," they whispered to themselves. However, the Union foragers were not there for them. Instead, they took all the bread, butter, cheese, milk and meat on the place and then moved on. No slaves ran away that day, but the extended McGee family was in no mood to accept that slavery was ending. For example, one of Boss's slaves ran away to the Union lines and then went back to get his sister. Unfortunately, Boss's brother-in-law William McGee found them and murdered the man. Later, two slaves from a nearby farm owned by a white man named Wallace were captured and hanged to death. Louis, Matilda and every other McGee slave were forced to see the hanged bodies and listen to every grisly detail of their capture and murder. Louis later remembered, "I never shall forget the horror of the scene—it was sickening. The bodies hung at the roadside, where the execution took place, until the blue flies literally swarmed around them, and the stench was fearful."

Back in Washington, the newly reelected president brooded over how to stop these horrors by passing the Thirteenth Amendment. Lincoln could wait until the new Congress was seated in March, but he wanted it passed and sent to the states as soon as possible. In December 1864, the president sent his annual message to Congress and urged them to pass the measure. On January 6, 1865, James M. Ashley of Ohio, a staunch Lincoln Republican, reintroduced the amendment in the House. Reaching out to border-state Unionists and moderate Democrats, the president argued that passage would convince the Confederacy that the border states would no longer prop up slavery and thus would hasten the end of the war. Lincoln told his allies to remind wavering House members that he was "president of the United States, clothed with great power. The abolition of slavery by constitutional provision settles the fate, for all coming time, not only of the millions now in bondage, but of unborn millions to come." On January 31, 1865, largely due to Lincoln's "great power," the House passed the measure and the amendment was sent to the states. Tennessee ratified the Thirteenth Amendment on April 7, 1865, but several more states were needed for it to be added to the Constitution. While the House of Representatives debated ending slavery, Louis and Matilda remained under the yoke of Sarah McGee. Fortunately for them, she was no longer the same person. The death of her husband and the collapse of her way of life weighed heavily on her. Louis noticed that "she was sadly changed….Her troubles and sorrows had crushed her former cruel and haughty spirit." Although it was clear to nearly everyone that slavery was finished, Madam and Old Master Jack clung ever more tightly to their chattel. No one was allowed to leave the property, and they were watched more closely. As the summer of 1865 began, Louis's friend and fellow slave George Washington learned that the McGees were no longer allowing slaves from nearby farms to visit their place. The McGees must have known that the Confederate government had dissolved and most of the Confederate armies had surrendered, but still they refused to let their

Louis Hughes escaped to Memphis in June 1865 and was shocked to see how large the city had grown.

slaves go. Louis and George Washington decided now was the time to strike for Memphis. On the afternoon of Sunday, June 25, Louis and George snuck through the orchard and left the McGee place. Shortly before the sun went down, they reached Senatobia, Mississippi, where they spent the night. It had all been rather uneventful. Rebel guerrillas were long gone, and Union soldiers were mostly indifferent to their plight. The following morning, they crept toward Hernando, which they reached early in the afternoon. Trains had ceased running in that part of Mississippi, but flat cars were being driven like wagons, and the two runaways joined one of these caravans. After several miles of difficult travel, Louis and George Washington arrived in Memphis around 7:00 p.m.

Louis could not believe how Memphis had changed. The old McGee home was now Union army headquarters, and the city was filled with Black people who cheered him as he walked the streets in amazement at the city's growth. The two men visited a Union official in hopes of getting an army escort to help them free their wives. Refusing to provide assistance, the official suggested they secure the help of some off-duty soldiers. The next morning, Louis and George Washington hired a wagon to go to the Union camp at Senatobia, where they hoped to find some willing soldiers. Stopping at Big Springs for the night, two soldiers approached their camp. "Have you any whiskey?" they asked. Sharing their liquor, Louis told them of their plight. In exchange for a bottle of whiskey, the soldiers agreed to give them the names of two comrades in Senatobia who would oblige them. The next day, Louis and George found the soldiers in camp, who agreed to help them. The party left Senatobia at 11:30 a.m., one week after Louis and George Washington had escaped. As the wagon driven by two Black men and flanked by two Union soldiers moved through the countryside, they passed several white farmers who watched them with hate in their eyes. When they cantered into the yard, the soldiers asked for horse feed, which Madam's brother William McGee refused to give them. Just then, Louis and George drove in. Shocked at what he saw, young McGee ran into the house screaming, "It is Louis and George, and I'll kill one of them to-night." The object of this threat paid little heed and instead loaded the wagon with their belongings and gathered Matilda and George's wife, Kitty, for the return to Memphis. Matilda's sister Mary Ellen joined them, and as they pulled out, she said, "Goodbye; I wish you good luck." In reply, Mrs. Farrington screamed, "I wish you all the bad luck!"

The ragged crew arrived back in Memphis on the Fourth of July, when "hundreds of colored refugees thronged the streets. Everywhere you looked you could see soldiers. Such a day I don't believe Memphis will ever see again—when so large and so motley a crowd will come together." After briefly taking in this spectacle, Louis found a place for them to stay, and two days later, he found a job driving a public carriage. His plan was to save his money so they could move to a Northern state. This desire was heightened when he learned from a family friend that Matilda's mother was living in Cincinnati, Ohio.

After spending six weeks in Memphis, Louis, Matilda and Mary Ellen left for Cincinnati. Trepidation turned to joy when Matilda found not only her mother but also one of her sisters. No rooms were available, so they moved to Hamilton, Ohio, where Louis worked odd jobs and the ladies took in laundry. On Christmas Day 1865, the entire family moved to Windsor, Canada, where they hoped for a better life free of the bitter legacy of slavery. Two weeks before Louis and his family arrived in Canada, Ann George was brought to Memphis by her owner. She may have been the last slave to come to Memphis before the institution was abolished. A week after she arrived, the Thirteenth Amendment was ratified by the required number of states, and slavery was finally finished. A week or so after Christmas, Ann George was set free. What would happen to her, Mary Herndon, Louis and Matilda Hughes and the thousands of other freed slaves remained to be seen as 1865 ended.

Chapter 5

"ALL THAT I HAD LEFT TO REMEMBER YOU"

1866–1956

When Ann George was set free, she secured a place to live and went to work for a white man named Wilson who toiled in a cigar shop. She cooked and washed for him, his wife and three children and tried to make ends meet while her husband was away working on a riverboat. In the early months of 1866, Robert Church Sr. was operating a saloon on DeSoto Street, Austin Cotton and James E. Donahue were working as carpenters, Hannah Robinson was a seamstress, Elvira Walker made her living washing clothes and Joseph Walker worked on the levee. The city where they lived and worked was growing more dangerous by the minute. Many whites, especially those of Irish descent, despised the former slaves and blamed them for their defeat in the war. As the author wrote in *A Brief History of Memphis*, "Many Irish Memphians felt deeply threatened by the large number of African Americans pouring into the city and feared that they might dislodge them as the city's most powerful ethnic group.... The Irish-dominated police force constantly mistreated black Memphians, while Irish laborers attempted to prevent African Americans from working in skilled trades." According to Donahue, "Whenever a policeman arrested a colored man, the first thing he did was to strike him." Another former slave, Prince Moultrie, stated that those who hated Black citizens were "the low down class among the Irish; I think they are about as mean a people as we have got here."

After a violent altercation on May 1 between police officers and former Black soldiers, armed whites moved into African American neighborhoods,

Former slaves sought assistance from the Memphis office of the Freedmen's Bureau.

killing anyone they could find. Joseph Walker left his job at the levee and was heading home when he saw an armed mob of citizens and police traveling down South Street. To avoid them, he turned toward the track and cars of the Tennessee and Mississippi Railroad depot. A white railroad agent named Palmer spotted Walker and ordered him to stop. When he refused, Palmer jerked his pistol and opened fire. Struck with one bullet, Walker ran home, but not before witnessing Palmer murder another Black man. Later that day, Austin Cotton was walking to his home behind John Hollywood's grocery store when a police officer ordered him to stop. Instead, Cotton started to run. A police officer yelled, "Halt you damn n----r, or we will knock you on the head." A white man grabbed him by the waist, and the officer pistol whipped him. Cotton soon broke away and ran into Hollywood's store. According to John Hollywood, as Cotton "got into the door, three or four men got hold of him and were licking him with pistols. I begged them to have some mercy on him and asked them not to kill the man in my own house." Cotton then broke free and escaped through the back of Hollywood's home. Outside Hollywood's door, a larger white mob attacked and murdered a drayman named Jackson Goodell. James Donahue was unharmed during the massacre, but he did witness acts of violence directed toward African Americans. Walking through an alleyway, he saw three police officers indiscriminately firing their pistols at a home occupied by Black women and children. As they pulled their triggers, Donahue heard them scream "that they were going to kill every damned n----r in Memphis." On the first evening of the massacre, Robert R. Church was standing in front of his house at 132 Monroe Street with a group of others. There they witnessed a mob of police officers beating an elderly Black man, who fortunately was able to slip from their grasp. On the third and final day of the disturbance, a mob of police, including officer Dave Roach, invaded Church's saloon and shot him in the neck. They drank their fill of his whiskey, destroyed the rest and stole $240 out of his money box. During his testimony to a congressional inquiry into the violence, Church was asked, "How much of a colored man are you?" He replied, "I do not know—very little; my father is a white man; my mother is as white as I am....My father owned my mother."

Hannah Robinson was in her house at Gayoso Street with her husband, son-in-law and sick daughter when twenty armed white men, including police officer Roach and a man named Chambers, burst through her door. "Get up, you God-damned n----rs and give us your arms!" Robinson told them they had no weapons, so the white men broke open her trunk, scattered her belongings and stole twenty-five dollars. They seized her husband's pocketbook and knife, and then, in an act of wanton cruelty, members of the mob smashed the bed her sick daughter was lying on. A few days later, she was dead. Elvira Walker was also sitting at home when she heard a knock on her door. A group of white men demanded to search her home for weapons. Finding none, they robbed her of a forty-five-dollar pocket watch, and one man sexually assaulted her by putting "his hands into my bosom." In the adjoining room were Peter and Rebecca Ann Bloom. The couple was lying in their bed when the mob burst through. The room was dark, and when Peter told them he had no candle, they went with him to find a light while a single terrorist was left to guard Rebecca Ann. She later testified, "He wanted to know if I had anything to do with white men. I said no. He held a knife in his hand and said that he would kill me if I did not let him do as he wanted to. I refused. He said, 'By God, you must,' and then he got into bed with me and violated my person, by having connexion with me, he still holding the knife." Ann George watched as fires consumed many buildings near her home and the residence of her employer, Wilson. One night, she watched a group of six men burn down a Black-operated tavern or "shebang" near her work. As the building caught fire, she heard one of the men call for a "Captain Wilson." Nervous about working for an arsonist, Ann told Wilson that she was going to move away because it was "getting too dangerous to stay there." Wilson replied that there was no reason to go. "We could have burned your house down last night if we had wanted to. I knew you were working for my wife, and I would not let you get into trouble. We had an order to burn down these houses." She did not ask who gave those orders and didn't really care. Soon after the massacre was over, Wilson left Memphis for Louisiana, and Ann George went to live and work for a Mr. Marsh. After three days of wanton killing and destruction, forty-six Black Memphians lay dead; Rebecca Ann Bloom and four other African American women had been raped; and ninety-one Black homes, twelve schools and four churches had been burned to the ground.

The cries of the dead hovered over the streets of Memphis for years to come. Black survivors vowed never to forget, while whites could not move fast enough to erase the memory of what they had done. However, many whites who did not participate in the massacre joined with Black leaders in creating a political coalition that led to former slaves being elected to public office. These included Joseph Clouston Sr., who was born on January 14, 1814, to Betsey McCabe and Scottish immigrant King Adams. Sold to Edward Clouston, he purchased his freedom in the 1840s and was able to

Ann George watched in horror as a mob led by her white employer burned down Black homes and schools in May 1866.

secure a job as a porter on a steamboat line, where, among other things, he learned to cut men's hair. By 1850, he had opened a barbershop in Memphis and purchased $650 in real estate. Ten years later, he owned $20,000 worth of real estate, and his personal property was valued at $1,200. After the war, Clouston went into the grocery business as well as continuing to own real estate valued at $10,000. In 1873, he was elected to the city's board of common council, where he served until 1876. When he died in 1895, he was mourned as "a man that every young man, regardless of race or color, should attempt to emulate." Lymus Wallace served on the school board and was elected to the city council in 1882. He also served on the board of education, and in 1887, he traveled to Washington, D.C., with the mayor and other local dignitaries to meet with President Grover Cleveland and invite him to visit Memphis. When Cleveland arrived in Memphis, Wallace was a member of the welcoming party. He was also a staunch defender of African American rights. When he learned during the flood of 1897 that white relief efforts were ignoring the plight of Blacks, Wallace formed his own relief committee that met the needs of hundreds of African American flood victims. In addition, he championed the building of a home for destitute former slaves that never fully got off the ground. In his later years, Wallace served as the manager of the Merchants and Planters Labor Agency, helping Black Memphians find jobs, until his death in 1918.

In Windsor, Canada, Louis and Matilda Hughes found work at the Iron House Hotel, but the wages were so low that Louis quit and found a job as a waiter at the Biddle House, located across the river in Detroit, Michigan. Two years later, he went to work as a sailor on a steamship that ran from Escanaba, Michigan, to Green Bay, Wisconsin. One day, a fellow sailor told him, "I used to sail with a man named Billy Hughes, and he looked just like you." Hope filled Louis's heart with the possibility of being reunited with one of his brothers, but he did not know where to start looking. When winter came and the sailing season ended, the steamer slipped into the port of Chicago, and Louis was left without work. While searching for a job, he ran into his old friend Thomas, who had escaped to Canada years before. Now named Thomas Bland, he helped Louis find work at the Sherman House, where he also worked. Meanwhile, back in Windsor, Matilda gave birth to two girls while still living with her mother, two sisters and their children. Once Matilda was healthy enough for travel, she joined her husband in Chicago, where they lived for several years. Respected for his professionalism and organizational skill, Louis was offered a position with the Plankinton House in Milwaukee, Wisconsin, which he accepted in the summer of 1868. He was placed in charge of the coat room and eventually also managed the bell stand. Matilda also held a management position at the Plankinton House; she was in charge of the sleeping apartments used by the hotel waiters. One afternoon, Louis was walking across the lobby when he suddenly saw Old Master Jack's son-in-law Colonel Hunting, who was visiting the North with his family. Being a free man afforded Louis the opportunity to determine how he would treat his former owners. In this instance, he decided to be gracious. He introduced himself to Hunting, who was pleased to see him. They shook hands, and each gathered their families for a proper reunion. When they parted, the McGees wished Louis and Matilda success with their new lives. Not long after, Louis was reunited with someone far more important to him.

Guests loved to talk with Louis, who regaled them with stories about his life as a slave. During one of these conversations, a white man asked him if he had a brother. When he replied yes, the man said, "Well, if you have a brother he is in Cleveland. There is a fellow there who is chief cook at the Forest City Hotel who looks just like you." Louis told the man that his brother's name was Billy and had a missing forefinger. Armed with this information, he promised to make contact when next in Cleveland. Louis was excited to the point of distraction, but he waited patiently until the man returned from Cleveland with confirmation that his brother was indeed alive and well. Securing leave, Louis made his way to Ohio, where he enjoyed a happy reunion with his brother and met his sister-in-law and their children. Billy explained he had gone back to Virginia after the war in hopes of finding their mother and brother but was unsuccessful. Ever since he had been cruelly ripped from the arms of his mother, Louis had felt alone in this world. Not even the love of Matilda and his girls fully assuaged his loneliness. With at least some of his family ties restored, Louis found a sense of peace that remained with him for the rest of his life. Louis Hughes eventually became a nurse, and in 1897, he wrote and published his autobiography, titled *Thirty Years a Slave: From Bondage to Freedom*. Ten years after his book appeared, Matilda died, and in 1913, the extraordinary life of Louis Hughes came to an end.

While Louis and Matilda Hughes were living and working in Milwaukee, Henry Davidson continued to live with his former owner's family and attend First Methodist Church. When he died in 1908, Henry was staying in the home of Thomas Davidson Lawler, the grandson of Thomas P. Davidson. As we will see, it was common for the white newspapers to portray former slaves as humble and simple people, loyal to their former owners and grateful for the treatment they received from them, while ex-owners were depicted as being kind and selfless toward their former property. However, in Henry Davidson's case, the evidence suggests there was genuine love and respect shared between him and his white family. Not only was he taken care of by multiple generations of the Davidson family, but he also continued to attend First Methodist Church, even after Collins Chapel was founded for African Americans to worship. The pastor of First Methodist, Reverend Lewis Powell, conducted Henry's funeral service, and the *Commercial Appeal* wrote, "In his death the last living link between old Wesley Chapel and the First Methodist Church…was broken and yesterday afternoon the body of the aged Negro was followed to a grave in Elmwood Cemetery by a score of his white friends, who paid him a final tribute of their love and affection in tears and floral offerings.…Side by side, the Negro, who under his black skin carried a noble heart, labored with his owner in founding the little chapel." To be sure, a whiff of paternalism clings to these words, but at the same time, there is reason to view the sentiments as heartfelt.

Mary Herndon was not as fortunate as Henry Davidson and Louis Hughes. She was a field hand and thus had no skills to build a better life, so she probably became a sharecropper, picking cotton as she had as a slave. Not much is known of what happened to her until 1933, when newspaper reporter J.H. Curtis found her in Memphis and interviewed her for the *Commercial Appeal*. Most of the profile concerned her life as a slave, but she also left a glimpse of what her life was like as a free woman: "I never was hungry in my life until now. I haven't much to live on of my old white folks from Misouri and Mason."

After his wound healed, Robert Church Sr. rebuilt his saloon and invested in real estate. Operating saloons and brothels, Church's tenants made a great deal of money, and the rents he collected made Church a very wealthy man. The violence directed against him in 1866 did little to prevent him from following his white father's dictum to not "let anyone call you a n----r." Once, a white policeman manhandled Church, who jerked a derringer and fired a warning shot over the officer's head. Acquitted on a charge of assault with an intent to kill, Church soon became the most important Black economic and political leader in Memphis and was widely hailed as the South's first Black millionaire. Church also created a cultural and political dynasty through his real estate holdings on Beale Street and his distinguished children. Daughter Mary Church Terrell was one of the first Black women to graduate from college, and as a teacher in Washington, D.C., she became a nationally known civil rights and suffrage activist. Robert Church Jr. remained in Memphis for much of his life, where he also became nationally famous as a leader in the

Republican Party. According to historian Preston Lauterbach, "Beale Street ranks as the dynasty's crowning achievement. Thanks in large part to Robert Church's audacity, vision, and acumen, Beale Street became the Main Street of Black America, a site of monumental innovations, thrilling promise, and devastating tragedy that wrote the headlines, played the soundtrack, and forged the secret history of an era, unmatched in prowess by any three-block stretch in the land."

As Robert Church built his dynasty, waves of nostalgia for slavery and the Lost Cause of the Confederacy spread throughout the South in the 1880s and 1890s. Confederate monuments were built, Joel Chandler Harris's Uncle Remus African folktales delighted adults and children alike and the racist novels of Thomas Dixon Jr. stirred fear and hatred against former slaves and their children. In 1905, a statue of Nathan Bedford Forrest was erected in Memphis, and two years later, Confederate Park opened on the city's bluff overlooking the Mississippi River. Textbooks written or approved by the United Daughters of the Confederacy, which extolled the virtues of the Rebel South and downplayed the cruelty of slavery, were used in classrooms throughout the South. Despite all this, Black southerners knew the truth: slavery was an evil institution, and the noble Confederacy was little more than a morally hobbled state. The culture of the Lost Cause did more than obscure the truth; it laid the foundation for a series of laws and Supreme Court decisions that segregated and therefore denied full equality to ex-slaves and their posterity.

In the early 1880s, former slave Sallie J. Robinson purchased a first-class ticket to travel on the Memphis and Charleston Railroad. When she attempted to enter the ladies' car, a conductor grabbed her roughly by the arm and barred her from the car. Robinson was defended by William M. Randolph, a former Confederate district attorney who had served as Memphis city attorney from 1869 to 1874. Randolph argued that the treatment received by Robinson violated the Civil Rights Act of 1875, which granted her the right to equal treatment in public accommodations and transportation. The trial jury disagreed and found in favor of the railroad, so Randolph appealed to the United States Supreme Court. "The defendant…must allege and prove that denial was for some reason, and that such reason was in its nature applicable to citizens of every race and color, and regardless of any previous condition of servitude," pleaded Randolph. The court bundled the Robinson case with four similar arguments into what was collectively called the Civil Rights Cases. Handed down in October 1883, the court's decision overturned the Civil Rights

Act of 1875, declaring the Constitution does not grant Congress the power to prevent private entities from discriminating against anyone they wish. It based its ruling on the Tenth Amendment to the Constitution, which states, "The powers not delegated to the United States by the Constitution, nor prohibited by it to the States, are reserved to the States respectively, or to the people." In a statement that would haunt Black citizens for decades to come, the majority opinion explained that "when a man has emerged from slavery, and by the aid of beneficent legislation has shaken off the inseparable concomitants of that state, there must be some stage in the progress of his elevation when he takes the rank of a mere citizen, and ceases to be the special favorite of the laws, and when his rights as a citizen, or a man, are to be protected in the ordinary modes by which other men's rights are protected." In other words, Ann George, Henry Davidson, Mary Herndon, Louis Hughes and the millions of other former slaves could suffer unequal treatment and be legally segregated from their white neighbors. This was reiterated in 1896 when the Supreme Court ruled in favor of "separate but equal" public accommodations in its *Plessy v. Ferguson* decision, which declared, "If one race be inferior to the other socially, the Constitution of the United States cannot put them upon the same plane." Along similar lines, the Tennessee General Assembly passed the Hancock Law, which required segregated seating for Black and white citizens riding on public transportation.

Along with the veneration of Confederate soldiers, the white South also lionized the "faithful" slaves who accepted their place, remained loyal to their owners and continued to be humble and subservient as "free" men and women. From the 1890s to the 1930s, the Memphis *Commercial Appeal* newspaper often published stories about former slaves, holding them up as examples of how younger African Americans should comport themselves within a segregated society. In the fall of 1896, the *Commercial Appeal* published a story about a former slave named Turner Montgomery. Born in Virginia, he was torn from his parents and sold to the owner of a Mississippi plantation, where "he labored as a Negro lad through the years of the war, remaining faithful to his master's family, until the Emancipation Proclamation was given, Lee had surrendered, and the Confederacy fallen." He eventually made his way to Memphis, where he worked as a waiter at the Gayoso Hotel. One day, he struck up a conversation with one of the hotel's guests, a man named Black from St. Louis. As they talked, Black asked Turner where he was from and who had owned him. "Here Black manifested a characteristic of the majority of Southern people. The true Southerner likes the modest black Negro." Turner stated that he had once belonged to Captain Lewis Edmunds, and Black replied that he knew Edmunds's son Ben, whom Turner also remembered. Black promised to write Ben Edmunds in hopes of finding out what happened to his parents. Four months later, Turner Montgomery received a letter from his mother: "The mother tells Montgomery (no Mister for him) of his father's death which occurred 'years ago,' and she has 'since the war married again.' She concludes her letter by saying, 'I hope you will write to me then send me your photograph, and also come to see me….I still have my Bible with your age in it, as that was all that I had left to remember you."

Despite the paternalism and stereotyping, articles like these help us understand how slaves endured the brutality of slavery and what happened to them once they were emancipated. At times, we see how some former slaves became respected members of the Memphis community, while the memory of others was smothered by savage caricature. As we have seen, in 1850 seven-year-old David Jones, his mother, Matilda, and sisters Jane and Eveline were set free after the death of their owner, Caesar Jones. Matilda was described as having a "brown complexion," while David, Eveline and Jane were listed as mulattos. More than likely this means Caesar had either a consensual or forced sexual relationship with Matilda, and her three children were also his. When David turned eighteen, he joined the Confederate army as a body servant, eventually serving under Nathan Bedford Forrest. After the war ended, he returned to Memphis and opened a barbershop in the lobby of the Memphis National Bank, located at the corner of Monroe and Main Streets. In his 1897 obituary, the *Commercial Appeal* wrote, "His life was upright, his business conduct above reproach, and he had a history that drew to him and held a patronage from gentlemen of the old school." It went on to describe his barbershop as "the place where members of the legal profession, rich merchants, and professional men went to have their barbering done by an old time Southern Negro." Edmund Turley also served as a Confederate body servant to his owner, Thomas Battle Turley. Edmund participated in the Battles of Shiloh, Atlanta and Nashville, where he "became cook for the brigade in which his master was fighting. Repeatedly he was under fire with him." After the war, Edmund remained a servant of Thomas Battle, who was chosen United States senator from Tennessee in 1897 and served until 1901. In June 1905, Edmund died and was buried in the Turley family plot in Elmwood Cemetery. "This man was of a type which is rapidly disappearing forever from the South—a fact sadly evidenced by the passing reunions of Confederate veterans, at each of which a lessening number of white-headed old darkies mingle with their former masters and share in their affectionate reminiscences. There is no race problem with these."

In the June 13, 1907 edition of the *Commercial Appeal*, it was reported that "Susan Hays, a true type of the old-fashioned Southern 'mammy,' and who has been a servant in the family of W.A. Collier for many years, died yesterday." When Jane Nunn died in 1910 at the age of 109, her obituary noted that before her death, she was the oldest person living in Memphis. It ended by explaining that "the old darkey is survived by several children, who are said to be good Negroes. Her funeral will take place this afternoon at 2 o'clock in Elmwood cemetery." On May 26, 1927, Jim Scott filed suit in Shelby County Chancery Court to prevent two white men from desecrating the grave of his former owner, Dr. John W. Scott. Gus McCulough and T.T. Skinner purchased land next to the Scott burial ground and planned to plow up the grave site along with their own land. The obituary for Union army veteran Horace Mayweathers was far more respectful and devoid of racist imagery. He was described as "an aged Memphis Negro" who fought "with the federal Army until the close of the war, when he was given an honorable discharge." On his 97th birthday, July 4, 1932, the *Commercial Appeal* published an interview with Henry Gamble Burford, a former slave and Union army veteran. Burford described life on the plantation before the war and his service as a soldier, which regrettably was transcribed by the white reporter in a thick dialect. "Shucks, on ol' Marse Burford's place, we growed wheat, we growed rye an' oats an' corn, an' we had hogs an' cows, an' sheep, an' tobaccy….In six year on Marse Burford's place dey wasn't a killing or a meanness amongst all dem darkies. Darkies didn't fight wid razors and guns and carry on like dey do now." In explaining his war service, Burford said, "We sojered for three years in and out o' Memphis and fit some battles. I was in one big un in Mississippi, I done forgot de name of de place. We had to fight hard, because de C'nfed'rates didn't have no love for cullud sojers." Finally, Burford was asked to comment on the Great Depression: "Folks don't grow enough to eat. Dey growed more to eat in one year in slavery time den day grows in 10 year now." To be sure, all of these stories in some way mythologize slavery, but the truth was sometimes revealed. When Mary Herndon described being beaten with a hoe by her owner's wife and Henry Gamble Burford explained that Rebels "had no love" for Black soldiers, reality does shine through.

Unfortunately, most white Memphians preferred the myth to the truth, and as time went by, even the landmarks that witnessed slavery's brutality were wiped away. When Nathan Bedford Forrest sold his slave market in

Left: In 1956, the Tennessee Historical Commission placed this historic marker at the site of Forrest's slave market but did not mention it in the text.

Below: The children of former slaves faced an uncertain future as segregation and white devotion to the Lost Cause were used to restrict their liberty.

1861, the buildings were converted into the Hardwick House Hotel, and then, in the early twentieth century, the property was abandoned. In 1929, what was left of the market was torn down, and four modern one-story brick stores were erected on the site. Eventually, it became a paid parking lot serving visitors to the Shelby County Courthouse and members of Calvary

Episcopal Church. In 1956, the Tennessee Historical Commission placed several historical markers in Memphis, including one at the Forrest market. In an act of willful obfuscation, the marker did not include any reference to slavery. The evolution of the Forrest slave market property from a space for human trafficking to a place designed to regulate automobile traffic mirrors the removal of slavery from the memory and culture of Memphis and the United States. Blacks continued to live with the disabling effects of that awful system, while many whites simply ignored the past and its present-day consequences. But it would not always be so. In the second decade of the twenty-first century, a diverse group of Memphians gathered to remember and commemorate that which had been hidden for so long.

Epilogue

"PRAYERS FOR FORGIVENESS, HEALING AND RECONCILIATION"

The sun shined brightly on Memphis as several hundred people passed through the doors of Calvary Episcopal Church for a very special event. It was April 4, 2018, and across the city, Memphians were commemorating the fiftieth anniversary of Dr. Martin Luther King's assassination. Although Dr. King's message of love and nonviolence was an important part of the service, its purpose was to honor the enslaved of Memphis.

Founded in 1832, the church is located on North Second Street at Adams Avenue, right next door to the site of Nathan Bedford Forrest's slave market and jail. The fact that nineteenth-century parishioners walked by human suffering and did nothing about it weighed heavily on the twenty-first-century congregation. This was especially true for Timothy S. Huebner, a distinguished history professor at Rhodes College. Huebner was troubled by the 1956 historical marker located on the market site that purposely obscured Forrest's buying and selling of human beings. Glossing over his trading in slaves, the marker referred to it simply as "business enterprises." In the fall of 2017, Huebner assigned one of his history classes to research Forrest's slave business and to then use the findings to compose a more accurate historical marker. Partnering with Tim Good of the National Park Service and the church, Huebner was able to secure the marker and schedule an unveiling for the spring of 2018. Reverend Scott Walters, Huebner and the rest of the clergy organized "a service of remembrance and reconciliation" to bring attention to Forrest's "business enterprises" and the people enslaved by his

A second marker was placed at the site in 2018 that explained in detail Forrest's involvement in the slave trade.

entrepreneurial spirit. Scripture was read, music was played, a sermon was given and a "litany of prayers for forgiveness, healing and reconciliation" was offered.

Then a remarkable thing happened. As the names of seventy-two slaves were read aloud, the six hundred members of the audience quietly and spontaneously stood in honor of those whose suffering had done much to build Memphis but were then erased from its history. Reverend Walters later wrote:

> *Someone at the back of the church stood up after maybe a dozen names had been read. And, one after another, the rest of us rose in response. We became a slow and reverent wave that moved from the back of the Calvary nave to the front....A spirit...or rather, the Spirit moved among us. The necessary work of the people became clear to us only in that moment. We stood, and wept, and paid whatever long overdue respects we could to the lives behind the names.*

Later, the congregation walked outside to unveil the marker, which reads in part:

> *From 1854 to 1860, Nathan Bedford Forrest operated a profitable slave trading business at this site....Much of the slave trade in Memphis occurred on Adams Avenue. Located in the heart of town and connecting the riverfront steamboat landing to the Memphis and Charleston Railroad line, the street offered easy access to buyers and sellers. In 1855, the city directory listed eight slave dealers, including Forrest, five of whom were located on Adams.*

The marker also contains a quote from Horatio Eden describing the slave market and details Forrest's involvement in the illegal international slave trade. Today, both markers stand silently near one another, one perpetuating a lie and the second a symbol of truth and reconciliation.

Perhaps now Henry Davidson, Louis and Matilda Hughes, Ann George, Mary Herndon and the thousands of other slaves who lived and died in Memphis can rest a bit easier knowing they have not been forgotten.

Appendix

LIST OF MEMPHIS AND SHELBY COUNTY SLAVES

Aaron: about 25 years old, 5 feet 6 or 8 inches tall. "He is black and speaks slow, small eyes, lame in his left hand when he went off so he could not shut it and kept it wrapped up." Ran away from J.L. Brooks on February 10, 1839.

Aaron: arrested on February 12, 1859, for "got boy Bill to steal from Stephens; no money." Owned by James Deloney.

Abb: about 30 years old. "Pursuant to a decree of Chancery Court, at Memphis, rendered November term 1858, in the case of Newton Ford, Administrator of Thomas Mull, deceased, and others, vs. John S. Clayton and others, creditors of Thomas Mull, deceased, I will on Tuesday February 1, 1859, in front of my office, in the City of Memphis, proceed to sell to the highest bidder, for cash." Clerk and master John C. Lanier.

Abner: owned by Bolton, Dickens and Co. and sold to Duffy on January 23, 1857.

Abraham: "19 years old, dark complexion, weighs 130 or 140 pounds." Owned by James Wall of Louisville. Arrested by the Shelby County sheriff for being a runaway on September 30, 1839.

Adaline and her child: owned by Thomas Dickens and sold to Bolton, Dickens and Co. on February 9, 1857.

Adam: about 50 years old. "Pursuant to a decree of Chancery Court, at Memphis, rendered November term 1858, in the case of Newton Ford, Administrator of Thomas Mull, deceased, and others, vs. John S. Clayton and others, creditors of Thomas Mull, deceased, I will on

Tuesday February 1, 1859, in front of my office, in the City of Memphis, proceed to sell to the highest bidder, for cash." Clerk and master John C. Lanier.

Adam Lock: plasterer. About sixty-seven years old in 1866.

Adam Setters: owned by Bolton, Dickens and Co. and sent by J. Guest.

Agnes Faro: owned by Bolton, Dickens and Co. Sent to G.L. Bumpass of Lexington, Kentucky, on November 18, 1856.

Agnus: owned by Bolton, Dickens and Co. and sent by Carmon to Arkansas River.

Ailcey: about sixty years old. "Pursuant to a decree of the Chancery Court at Memphis, rendered at the November term, 1858, in the case of Lucy W. Stark, administratrix of Henry C. Stark, deceased, and others, vs. Margaret Stark, Louisiana Farabee, and others, creditors of Henry C. Stark, deceased, I will on Thursday, the 25th of January, 1859, at the late residence of Henry C. Stark, deceased, in Shelby county, Tennessee, near Fisherville, proceed to sell to the highest bidder." Clerk and master John C. Lanier.

Albert: arrested for "fighting; had $1.75" on September 19, 1859. Owned by Ray.

Albert: arrested for "flask of whiskey; had $1.75" on January 3, 1860. Owned by R.T. Toryan.

Albert: arrested on February 12, 1859, for "got boy Jiles to steal." Owned by Brunson Bayliss.

Albert: arrested on February 22, 1859, for "fighting; hired by Dr. Edmund; no money." Owned by Brunson Bayliss.

Albert: arrested on February 23, 1860, for "no pass." Owned by Woodson.

Albert: owned by Bolton, Dickens and Co. Sent to G.L. Bumpass of Lexington, Kentucky, on December 18, 1856.

Alcy Vaden: owned by Bolton, Dickens and Co. and sent by J. Guest.

Alec: about eleven years old. "Pursuant to a decree of the Chancery Court at Memphis, rendered at the November term, 1858, in the case of Lucy W. Stark, administratrix of Henry C. Stark, deceased, and others, vs. Margaret Stark, Louisiana Farabee, and others, creditors of Henry C. Stark, deceased, I will on Thursday, the 25th of January, 1859, at the late residence of Henry C. Stark, deceased, in Shelby county, Tennessee, near Fisherville, proceed to sell to the highest bidder." Clerk and master John C. Lanier.

Alexander: "about 45 years old, 6 feet tall, about 180 pounds, square shoulders, long arms, small legs and large feet, missing some of his teeth, small eyes, and a disfigured thumbnail." Ran away from owner R. Payne at the end of April 1839.

Alexander: sold by auctioneer J.E. Phillips on March 11, 1846, at the Commercial Hotel.

Alfred: arrested for being "disorderly; had $2.20 & knife" on December 29, 1859. Owned by Captain Church.

Alfred: arrested for "beating his team unmercifully; had $70" on January 16, 1859. Owned by the Gayoso House.

Alfred: owned by Bolton, Dickens and Co. and sold to Saul Hawkins of Vicksburg, Mississippi, on September 24, 1856. Swapped for Sarah.

Alfred Leucose: owned by Bolton, Dickens and Co. and sold to G.W. Babcock.

Alice: about ten years old. "Pursuant to a decree of the Chancery Court at Memphis, rendered at the November term, 1858, in the case of Lucy W. Stark, administratrix of Henry C. Stark, deceased, and others, vs. Margaret Stark, Louisiana Farabee, and others, creditors of Henry C. Stark, deceased, I will on Thursday, the 25th of January, 1859, at the late residence of Henry C. Stark, deceased, in Shelby county, Tennessee, near Fisherville, proceed to sell to the highest bidder." Clerk and master John C. Lanier.

Alice: ran away from J.W. Crisp and Co. on February 5, 1861. "Mulatto or quadroon woman, weighing about one hundred and twenty pounds, well-formed and good looking, about eighteen years old, having large, full, dark eyes, black hair, not kinkey, but inclined to curl and large broad front teeth, not very white, with considerable space between them."

Allen Price: owned by Bolton, Dickens and Co. and sold to Duffy on January 23, 1857.

Ally Ann: owned by Bolton, Dickens and Co. and sold to Saul Hawkins of Vicksburg, Mississippi, on September 24, 1856.

America: owned by Bolton, Dickens and Co. Sent to G.L. Bumpass of Lexington, Kentucky, on December 18, 1856.

Amos: "19 or 20 years old, yellow complexion, 5 feet 2 or 3 inches tall, slow in speech." Ran away from owner William R. Greenlaw. "I expect said boy will try to get on a boat either at Memphis or Randolph, to get to a free state."

Andrew: arrested for being a runaway on July 5, 1843. "Andrew is black, 5 feet 8 inches high, rather slim, will weigh about 135 lbs., 22 years old, several front teeth missing, and slow spoken." Owned by the estate of Wright Elliott, deceased of Marion, Arkansas, and hired by Alexander McNeil of LaGrange, Tennessee, for the present year.

Andy: in February 1854 Gallows Construction Company paid for his services and in 1858 sold at auction from Thomas Mull to F. Lane; about thirty-five years old.

Ann: sold by Clerk and Master John C. Lanier on June 1, 1859. "Pursuant to a decree of the Chancery Court at Memphis, rendered November Term, 1858, in the case of William and Mary Braswell and Elizabeth Braswell vs. Benjamin Askew and D.M. Sanderlin. In front of my office, in the city of Memphis, proceed to sell to the highest bidder for cash."

Ann: "20 or 22 years-old, 5 feet 4 or 5 inches tall, very quick spoken and speaks somewhat broken." Arrested for being a runaway slave and housed in the Shelby County Jail on October 26, 1838.

Ann Eliza: owned by Bolton, Dickens and Co. and sold to Saul Hawkins of Vicksburg, Mississippi, on September 24, 1856.

Ann Hickson: owned by Bolton, Dickens and Co. and sent by J. Guest.

Ann Jackson: owned by Thomas Dickens and sold to Bolton, Dickens and Co. on February 9, 1857.

Ann Manab: owned by Thomas Dickens and sold to Bolton, Dickens and Co. on February 9, 1857.

Ann Patrick Ayr: owned by a Mr. Patrick for seventeen years. Came to Memphis in 1847 or 1848.

Annita: "excellent general hand 25 years old." Sold by J.E. Phillips in front of the Commercial Hotel on February 19, 1846.

Anny: about three years old. "Pursuant to a decree of the Chancery Court at Memphis, rendered at the November term, 1858, in the case of Lucy W. Stark, administratrix of Henry C. Stark, deceased, and others, vs. Margaret Stark, Louisiana Farabee, and others, creditors of Henry C. Stark, deceased, I will on Thursday, the 25th of January, 1859, at the late residence of Henry C. Stark, deceased, in Shelby county, Tennessee, near Fisherville, proceed to sell to the highest bidder." Clerk and master John C. Lanier.

Armstead: fifteen or sixteen years old, five feet tall. Owned by Mr. Booker of Somerville, Tennessee. Arrested on May 8, 1839, by the Shelby County sheriff for being a runaway slave.

Arthur: arrested for being a runaway from Benjamin Polk, of Yalobusha County, Mississippi, on April 7, 1859. "About 21 years old; black complexion; will weigh about 150 lbs.; two scars on his right wrist; no other marks visible."

Balinda: on June 14, 1860, "put up for safe keeping" by owner and policeman N.L. Laurence.

Baner: about five years old. "Pursuant to a decree of the Chancery Court at Memphis, rendered at the November term, 1858, in the case of Lucy W. Stark, administratrix of Henry C. Stark, deceased, and others, vs. Margaret Stark, Louisiana Farabee, and others, creditors of Henry C. Stark, deceased, I will on Thursday, the 25th of January, 1859, at the late residence of Henry C. Stark, deceased, in Shelby county, Tennessee, near Fisherville, proceed to sell to the highest bidder." Clerk and master John C. Lanier.

Ben Bangor: owned by Bolton, Dickens and Co. Sent to G.L. Bumpass of Lexington, Kentucky, on December 18, 1856.

Ben Banjo Player: owned by Bolton, Dickens and Co. and sold to Hawkins on December 19, 1856.

Ben Bone: owned by Bolton, Dickens and Co. Sent to G.L. Bumpass of Lexington, Kentucky, on December 18, 1856.

Ben Boyer: owned by Bolton, Dickens and Co.

Ben Bryer: owned by Bolton, Dickens and Co. and sold to G.W. Babcock.

Betty: sold by the Shelby County sheriff on February 18, 1859. "By virtue of an execution issued from the Circuit Court of Shelby County, in favor of R.E. Orne, vs. John Coleman, R.T.G. Hart, et. al., issued 19th September 1858."

Bill: "about 25 years old, 5 feet six inches high, of very dark complexion, high forehead with some of his front teeth out, when spoken to he answers quickly and wears a smiling countenance, weighs about 100 pounds. Owned by Thomas Mackey, executor of the estate of John Best, dec'd," and stolen on January 10, 1836.

Bill: twenty years old on January 14, 1859. "The Corporation charging more than I am able to pay for license, having been totally raised to about eight hundred dollars, including auction and negro license, brought forward by one of our city fathers in the same business as myself, so I have been told, but it is immaterial who was the originator of the outrageous tax, I for one, cannot pay it, therefore I wish to change my business, and will sell all the negroes on hand low for cash."

Bill Trezevant: ran away from W. Fitzgerald of Senatobia, Mississippi, on February 3, 1859. "About thirty-one years old, black, has a heavy beard, and some marks of the lash upon his back. He has been employed at the Worsham House, Commercial Hotel, and other places in Memphis at different times for some years past, and is believed to be lurking somewhere in the neighborhood at present."

Bob: about twenty-four years old. "Pursuant to a decree of the Chancery Court at Memphis, rendered at the November term, 1858, in the case of

Lucy W. Stark, administratrix of Henry C. Stark, deceased, and others, vs. Margaret Stark, Louisiana Farabee, and others, creditors of Henry C. Stark, deceased, I will on Thursday, the 25th of January, 1859, at the late residence of Henry C. Stark, deceased, in Shelby county, Tennessee, near Fisherville, proceed to sell to the highest bidder." Clerk and master John C. Lanier.

Bob: arrested as a runaway on January 10, 1859. "About 17 or 18 years old; black color; about five feet high, and will weigh about 125 or 130 pounds; no scars or marks recollected." Owned by Daniel Butts of Fayette County, Tennessee.

Boston: arrested for being a runaway on October 18, 1859. Owned by Mrs. Doyle.

Bradly: arrested for being a runaway on December 13, 1859. "Dark complexion; weighs 165 or 170 pounds; 23 or 25 years old; 5 feet 8 or 10 inches high." Owned by Dr. John Sweden of Hickory Wythe, Tennessee.

Candice: about sixteen years old. "Pursuant to a decree of the Chancery Court at Memphis, rendered at the November term, 1858, in the case of Lucy W. Stark, administratrix of Henry C. Stark, deceased, and others, vs. Margaret Stark, Louisiana Farabee, and others, creditors of Henry C. Stark, deceased, I will on Thursday, the 25th of January, 1859, at the late residence of Henry C. Stark, deceased, in Shelby county, Tennessee, near Fisherville, proceed to sell to the highest bidder." Clerk and master John C. Lanier.

Candise: "25-year-old house servant, a member of likely family of Negroes." Auctioned by A.S. Levy and Company on April 28, 1859.

Carolina Whaley: owned by Bolton, Dickens and Co. Sent to G.L. Bumpass of Lexington, Kentucky, on November 18, 1856.

Caroline: about thirty years old. "Pursuant to a decree of Chancery Court, at Memphis, rendered November term 1858, in the case of Newton Ford, Administrator of Thomas Mull, deceased, and others, vs. John S. Clayton and others, creditors of Thomas Mull, deceased, I will on Tuesday February 1, 1859, in front of my office, in the City of Memphis, proceed to sell to the highest bidder, for cash." Clerk and master John C. Lanier.

Caroline: eleven years old on January 14, 1859. "The Corporation charging more than I am able to pay for license, having been totally raised to about eight hundred dollars, including auction and negro license, brought forward by one of our city fathers in the same business as myself, so I have been told, but it is immaterial who was the originator of the outrageous tax, I for one, cannot pay it, therefore I wish to change my business, and will sell all the negroes on hand low for cash."

Caroline: "filed as power of attorney; mulatto woman 45 years old." Sold in 1860.

Catherine: nineteen years old on January 14, 1859. "The Corporation charging more than I am able to pay for license, having been totally raised to about eight hundred dollars, including auction and negro license, brought forward by one of our city fathers in the same business as myself, so I have been told, but it is immaterial who was the originator of the outrageous tax, I for one, cannot pay it, therefore I wish to change my business, and will sell all the negroes on hand low for cash."

Cato: ran away from Charles Lofland on March 3, 1840. "He is black, about 5 feet 6 or 8 inches high, heavy built, between 28 and 30 years old, and generally wears a black fur hat with a narrow brim." "Was formerly the property of Rev. Mr. Alston. He has a wife in the neighborhood of Randolph, and may have gone there, or may be in this vicinity."

Cezer: arrested for "misdemeanor; had nothing" on November 30, 1860. Owned by William Richman.

Chantlin: "taken in by Patterson" on July 16, 1859. Owned by Dr. Ewing of Louisiana.

Charity: "black color aged about nineteen years." Used as mortgage collateral in 1860.

Charity: owned by Bolton, Dickens and Co. and sold to Duffy on January 23, 1857.

Charity: ran away from Pamela Childs on March 1, 1859. "Very smart and active, dark complexion, and 20 years of age."

Charles: ran away and was arrested on August 24, 1843. "Charles is quite black, 5 feet 9 inches high, about 25 years old; will weigh 150 lbs., and has a smart gap in his upper and under front teeth, but no front tooth missing." Owned by William Stephens of Hardeman County, Tennessee.

Charley: arrested on January 31, 1859, for being a runaway. "About seventeen or eighteen years old; five feet four inches high; weighs about 130 pounds." Owned by John B. Harring of Pontotoc County, Mississippi.

Chloe: forty years old with her five-month-old child. Available for hire from January 10, 1859, to January 1, 1860. Owned by M.C. Cayce.

Coty Young: owned by Bolton, Dickens and Co. Sent to G.L. Bumpass of Lexington, Kentucky, on November 18, 1856.

Crese: ran away from Patrick Meagher on October 26, 1827. "A likely negro girl, aged about sixteen years, with nose inclined to Roman. She has the ends from the third and fourth fingers of the right hand taken off by a burn, and is extremely forward and pert when spoken to."

Crockett: arrested on August 31, 1859, for fighting. Owned by A. Moore.

Croy: arrested for "tax not paid; Jimeson agent" on November 3, 1860. Owned by Grigrey.

Cuff: arrested on December 25, 1860, for "misdemeanor." Owned by George House.

Cuff: arrested on May 26, 1859, for "no pass after 9." Owned by J.J. Worsham.

Cuffy: arrested on April 26, 1859 for "drunk & disorderly." Owned by Worsham House.

Cynthia Townsend: lived in Memphis eighteen years in 1866. Bought her freedom a few days before Union forces seized Memphis.

Cyrus: sold at auction by G.B. Locke and Company on May 28, 1859. "33 years old, a No. 1 Cook and Dining-room Servant."

Daniel: about thirty years old. "Pursuant to a decree of Chancery Court, at Memphis, rendered November term 1858, in the case of Newton Ford, Administrator of Thomas Mull, deceased, and others, vs. John S. Clayton and others, creditors of Thomas Mull, deceased, I will on Tuesday February 1, 1859, in front of my office, in the City of Memphis, proceed to sell to the highest bidder, for cash." Clerk and master John C. Lanier.

Daniel: arrested on December 28, 1859, for "no pass." Owned by Mrs. Giles.

Daniel: arrested on December 30, 1860, for "misdemeanor; bundle of books & knife." Owned by Sasfferens.

Daniel: owned by Bolton, Dickens and Co. Sent to G.L. Bumpass of Lexington, Kentucky, on the steamer *Princess* on October 24, 1856.

Daniel H. Jones: slave pastor of First Methodist Church's Black congregation from November 3, 1851, until his death in 1854.

Dave: arrested for "running hack over a boy" on October 20, 1859. Owned by Judy Baker.

Dave: ran away from Nathan Bedford Forrest's slave yard "about the middle of December [1858]." "About five feet seven or eight inches high, dark copper complexion, and weighs about 160 or 170 pounds. Said negro was placed in my yard for sale by Dr. Robert Temple of Hernando, Miss., and lately belonged to Crawford Jones of Tunica County, Miss."

Davey No. 2: owned by Marmaduke Duke.

David: arrested on October 2, 1843, for being a runaway. "Tolerable black, of pleasant countenance, 5 feet 6 inches high, will weigh 140 lbs., and about 28 years old." Owned by Leshel Acker, of Panola County, Mississippi.

David: sold by Shelby County sheriff on June 11, 1836, for being an unclaimed runaway slave.

David Brown: owned by Bolton, Dickens and Co. and sold to Hawkins on December 19, 1856.

David Jones: born in 1843. Owned by Caesar A. Jones. Set free when Caesar Jones died in 1849. "Chamberlin Jones, executor of C.A. Jones, deceased—free papers of David, son of Matilda." Died in 1897.

Davy: owned by Bolton, Dickens and Co.

D.B. Banks: born in Virginia. Owned by a man named Moore who took him to Kentucky and then to Memphis. Died in 1929 at the age of eighty-six.

Delpha: arrested on October 2, 1843, for being a runaway. "Black 5 feet 8¼ inches high, about 35 years old, will weigh about 140 lbs., has lost the fore finger of the left hand to the first joint." Owned by Ire McKenny of Panola County, Mississippi.

Dick: "fine plough boy, 12 years old." Sold by J.E. Phillips in front of the Commercial Hotel on February 19, 1846.

Dick Saffler: owned by Bolton, Dickens and Co. Sent to G.L. Bumpass of Lexington, Kentucky, on November 18, 1856.

Dinah Johnston: owned by Bolton, Dickens and Co. and sent by J. Guest.

Docter: arrested for "no pass" on October 26, 1859. Owned by Goyer and Nealy.

Dolla: owned by Bolton, Dickens and Co. Sent to Memphis by Wade Bolton on March 24, 1857.

Dolphin: arrested on December 12, 1859, for "misdemeanor; had cards & knife." Owned by George Lincoln.

Dorcus: owned by Bolton, Dickens and Co. and sold to Saul Hawkins of Vicksburg, Mississippi, on September 24, 1856.

Drummer: arrested on December 22, 1858, for "drunk & disorderly." Owned by the estate of Judge Harris.

Drummond: fifty-year-old field hand. Available for hire from January 10, 1859, to January 1, 1860. Owned by M.C. Cayce.

Eadie: about twelve years old. "Pursuant to a decree of the Chancery Court at Memphis, rendered at the November term, 1858, in the case of Lucy W. Stark, administratrix of Henry C. Stark, deceased, and others, vs. Margaret Stark, Louisiana Farabee, and others, creditors of Henry C. Stark, deceased, I will on Thursday, the 25th of January, 1859, at the late residence of Henry C. Stark, deceased, in Shelby county, Tennessee, near Fisherville, proceed to sell to the highest bidder." Clerk and master John C. Lanier.

Easter: about fifteen years old. "Pursuant to a decree of the Chancery Court at Memphis, rendered at the November term, 1858, in the case of Lucy W. Stark, administratrix of Henry C. Stark, deceased, and others, vs. Margaret Stark, Louisiana Farabee, and others, creditors of Henry C. Stark, deceased, I will on Thursday, the 25th of January, 1859, at the late residence of Henry C. Stark, deceased, in Shelby county, Tennessee, near Fisherville, proceed to sell to the highest bidder." Clerk and master John C. Lanier.

Elisha Warfield: owned by Bolton, Dickens and Co. Sent to G.L. Bumpass of Lexington, Kentucky, on December 18, 1856.

Elizabeth: sold by auctioneer J.E. Phillips on March 11, 1846, at the Commercial Hotel.

Elizah Ross: owned by Bolton, Dickens and Co. and sold to Duffy on January 23, 1857.

Eliza Jane: ran away from John Williams on February 23, 1859. "Dark copper color, with right eye out; aged about thirty-eight years."

Eliza Robinson: owned by Bolton, Dickens and Co. "House negro" sent to Memphis by Jack Guest on April 23, 1857.

Eliza Ross: owned by Bolton, Dickens and Co. "House negro" sent to Memphis by Jack Guest on April 23, 1857.

Ell Agnew: committed to the Shelby County Asylum.

Ellen Love: sold to a man named Moon. In 1896, her sister Fannie Samuels of Hemstead County, Arkansas, wrote to the sheriff of Shelby County searching for her sister.

Elvira Walker: twenty-six years old in 1866.

Eugenie: about two years old. "Pursuant to a decree of the Chancery Court at Memphis, rendered at the November term, 1858, in the case of Lucy W. Stark, administratrix of Henry C. Stark, deceased, and others, vs. Margaret Stark, Louisiana Farabee, and others, creditors of Henry C. Stark, deceased, I will on Thursday, the 25th of January, 1859, at the late residence of Henry C. Stark, deceased, in Shelby county, Tennessee, near Fisherville, proceed to sell to the highest bidder." Clerk and master John C. Lanier.

Feildon: ran away from Mr. Ford of New Orleans. Arrested on May 22, 1839. "A likely negro man, of dark complexion, about 28 years of age, 5 feet 8 or 10 inches high, weighs about one hundred and seventy-five pounds."

Foster: arrested on August 7, 1859, for "living at Gayoso House without pass." Owned by Dr. Cooke.

Foster: arrested on June 17, 1859, for "running out; no pass." Owned by Gayoso House.

Frances: owned by Bolton, Dickens and Co. Sent to G.L. Bumpass of Lexington, Kentucky, on December 18, 1856.

Frances: owned by Bolton, Dickens and Co. Sent to G.L. Bumpass of Lexington, Kentucky, on the steamer *Princess* on October 24, 1856.

Gates Tom: owned by Bolton, Dickens and Co. and sold to Hodge on December 6, 1856.

General Jackson: owned by Bolton, Dickens and Co. and sold to Murfield on January 8, 1857.

George: "about 23 years old, yellow complexion, 5 feet 9 or 10 inches tall, weighs about 165 pounds." Owned by William White of Wilkinson County, Mississippi. Arrested by the Shelby County sheriff on November 5, 1838, for being a runaway slave. Sold on December 15, 1839.

George: arrested on April 14, 1839, for being a runaway. "A negro boy of dark complexion, about 10 or 12 years of age, 3 foot 4 or 5 inches high…says he belongs to Wm. McCarter who lives in Lowndes county, Miss., and says he was stolen from that place by a man named William Johnson."

George: arrested on December 16, 1858, for "at work on levee; no pass." Owned by Colonel Byrd Hill, who paid one dollar.

George: arrested on November 13, 1843, for being a runaway. "Quite black, 5 feet 6½ inches high, about 35 years old, will weigh 150 lbs., he has four small raised scars about one inch long each running across his breast." Owned by William Johnson of Richmond, Virginia.

George: arrested on November 15, 1843, for being a runaway. "Quite black, 5 feet 6¾ inches high, about 45 years old, will weigh 140 lbs., bald headed, front teeth scattering but none missing." Owned by Stephen Manor of Danville, Kentucky.

George: "22 or 23 years-old, 5 feet 2 or 3 inches tall, dark brown complexion, right ear missing." Arrested for being a runaway slave and held in the Shelby County Jail on November 6, 1838.

George Townsley: owned by Bolton, Dickens and Co. and sold to Duffy on January 23, 1857.

George Washington: owned by Bolton, Dickens and Co. and sold to Murfield on January 8, 1857.

George Williams: hack driver. Had a wife and thirteen-year-old child in 1866.

George Wise: "30 years old, 5 feet 8 or 10 inches, 150 pounds." Claimed to be a free man from Allegheny County, Pennsylvania, but was arrested by the Shelby County sheriff for being a runaway slave on May 22, 1839. Sold by the sheriff on July 6, 1840.

Giles: ran away from the Jackson Street south Memphis residence of William T. Williams on May 24, 1859. "About 40 years old, 5 feet high, dark complexion, bald head, and several front teeth out. He plays well on the banjo."

Grundy: arrested on August 7, 1843, for being a runaway. "Light complected 5 feet 9 inches high, 23 years old, will weigh 150 lbs, has a scar in the right eyebrow." Owned by Eli Anderson of Madison County, Tennessee.

Guss: four years old. "Pursuant to a decree of the Chancery Court at Memphis, rendered at the November term, 1858, in the case of Lucy W. Stark, administratrix of Henry C. Stark, deceased, and others, vs. Margaret Stark, Louisiana Farabee, and others, creditors of Henry C. Stark, deceased, I will on Thursday, the 25th of January, 1859, at the late residence of Henry C. Stark, deceased, in Shelby county, Tennessee, near Fisherville, proceed to sell to the highest bidder." Clerk and master John C. Lanier.

Hannah: arrested on June 8, 1860, for "runaway; put up/W. Cossey." Owned by Dr. Pittman.

Hannah: owned by Thomas Dickens and sold to Bolton, Dickens and Co. on February 9, 1857.

Hannah: ran away from George M. Penn on September 16, 1835. "About 40 years old, 5 feet 3 or 4 inches high, thick built, speaks low and but little, black complected, has a sulky appearance, bushy hair, and wore a blue domestic frock but had other clothes. Hannah left me with six other negroes, four of whom have since been taken in Arkansas on their way to a free State, and the other two were drowned. She is most probably in Arkansas making her way up the river."

Hannah George: twenty-nine years old in 1866. Came to Memphis in 1863. "My business is sewing, washing, and ironing."

Hannah Robinson: thirty-nine years old in 1866.

Hannah Savage: twenty-three years old in 1866.

Hannah Washington: owned by Bolton, Dickens and Co. and sent by J. Guess.

Hardy: arrested on April 30, 1859, for "no pass, no money." Owned by John Cubbins.

Harrell: owned by Bolton, Dickens and Co. and sent by Carmon to Arkansas River.

Harriet Armour: brought to Memphis by Mr. Merriweather in 1858 or 1860.

Harriett: about one year old. Sold by Thomas Mull to F. Lane.

Harriett: about twenty years old. "Pursuant to a decree of Chancery Court, at Memphis, rendered November term 1858, in the case of Newton Ford, Administrator of Thomas Mull, deceased, and others, vs. John S. Clayton and others, creditors of Thomas Mull, deceased, I will on Tuesday February 1, 1859, in front of my office, in the City of Memphis, proceed to sell to the highest bidder, for cash." Clerk and master John C. Lanier.

Harriett: fourteen years old on January 14, 1859. "The Corporation charging more than I am able to pay for license, having been totally raised to about eight hundred dollars, including auction and negro license, brought forward by one of our city fathers in the same business as myself, so I have been told, but it is immaterial who was the originator of the outrageous tax, I for one, cannot pay it, therefore I wish to change my business, and will sell all the negroes on hand low for cash."

Harriett: owned by Bolton, Dickens and Co. and sold to Saul Hawkins of Vicksburg, Mississippi, on September 24, 1856.

Harriett: owned by Thomas Dickens and sold to Bolton, Dickens and Co. on February 9, 1857.

Harriett: sold by Clerk and Master John C. Lanier on June 1, 1859. "Pursuant to a decree of the Chancery Court at Memphis, rendered November Term, 1858, in the case of William and Mary Braswell and Elizabeth Braswell vs. Benjamin Askew and D.M. Sanderlin."

Harriet Wilkerson: owned by Milton Berry and nursed his daughter Leila Scott Berry. She lived with Leila and her husband, John T. Willins, at 270 Beale Street until her death on November 16, 1898.

Harrison Davis: owned by Bolton, Dickens and Co. Sent to G.L. Bumpass of Lexington, Kentucky, on November 18, 1856.

Harry: arrested on September 8, 1859, for "suspicious pass; watch & 70 cents." Owned by E.H. Fager.

Henrietta: "good cook, washer, ironer, &c, 22 years old." Sold by J.E. Phillips in front of the Commercial Hotel on February 19, 1846.

Henrietta and her child: sold by James J. Baugh, administrator of the estate of Josiah Baugh, on March 11, 1846.

Henrietta Price: first former slave to file a last will and testament in Shelby County on February 22, 1866, where she left her property to her brothers and aunt.

Henry: "apprehended on the 25th of September [1827], by David Dunn, living on the north fork of Big Creek, Shelby county, Tennessee a mulatto boy, who calls himself Henry, about 14 years of age. He says he belongs to a Mr. Dunaway near Nashville, that he was bought of a Danl. White near Nashville, that Dunaway was taking him down the river to sell, and that he left him at the Flour Island Bluff about three or four weeks since."

Henry: arrested on October 3, 1843, for being a runaway. "Quite black, about 20 years old, 5 feet 3½ inches high, will weigh 125 lbs., he has a large scar from a burn between the elbow and shoulder of the right arm, and three scars from burns on the left arm." Owned by Jonathan Waters of Louisiana, near Vicksburg, Mississippi.

Henry: arrested on November 7, 1859, for gaming. "Yellow boy claims to be free."

Henry: owned by Bolton, Dickens and Co.

Henry: ran away from J.M.M. Cornelius of Germantown, Shelby County, Tennessee, on October 2, 1860. "A dark mulatto, with a full bushy head of hair and a large unshaven beard, above the medium height, intelligent, can read and write, and is very pompous in his language and actions, and about thirty years of age."

Henry or Harry: arrested on May 28, 1859, for "no pass after 9." Owned by Captain McManus.

Henry or Jack: "runaway slave from steamboat *Red River*" on December 29, 1858.

Henry Bond: drayman, freed in 1865.

Henry Gamble Burford: owned by Frank Mountain of Georgia and sold to the Burford plantation in Mississippi. Joined the Union army and served as a private in the Third Colored Artillery stationed in Memphis.

Henry Davidson: owned by Thomas P. Davidson.

Henry Dobson: owned by Bolton, Dickens and Co. and sent by J. Guest.

Henry Horne: owned by Thomas C. Horne. Brother of Willis and son of Kit Horne.

Henry Steen: owned by Thomas Dickens and sold to Bolton, Dickens and Co. on February 9, 1857.

Henry Talbot: owned by Bolton, Dickens and Co. Sent to G.L. Bumpass of Lexington, Kentucky, on November 18, 1856.

Isaac: "a very likely black fellow about twenty years of age, five feet six inches high, some small scars on his face." Owned by Durritt and Barnes. Ran away on September 30, 1836.

Isaac: died April 12, 1861, of drowning. Owned by Mr. Harrison and E. Levy.

Isaac: sold by auctioneer J.E. Phillips on March 11, 1846, at the Commercial Hotel.

Isaac Felder: owned by Bolton, Dickens and Co.

Isaac Thompson: sold by the Shelby County sheriff for being an unclaimed runaway slave on May 2, 1836.

Isack: arrested on September 26, 1860, for "leaving dray on sidewalk." Owned by Milese Owen.

Jack: "about 24 years old, 5 feet 10 inches tall, weighed 165 pounds." Owned by the Widow Cotton at LaGrange, Tennessee. Arrested on November 7, 1839, by the Shelby County sheriff.

Jack: arrested on May 25, 1860, for being "drunk; had $1.35 etc." Owned by W.L. Nelson.

Jack: arrested on October 15, 1860, for "misdemeanor; $25 bail." Owned by Mr. Lacy.

Jack: one of eight slaves arrested for attempted murder and burglary in 1832.

Jack: ran away from John McGrath in December 1858. "He is very black, about 6 feet two inches high, weighs about 180 pounds, has a scar over one of his eyes, and speaks in a fine voice; is a very smart boy, and has a long stride when he walks."

Jack Boyer: owned by Bolton, Dickens and Co. and sold to G.W. Babcock.

Jack Brown: owned by Bolton, Dickens and Co. Sent to G.L. Bumpass of Lexington, Kentucky, on December 18, 1856.

Jack Harris Walker: owned by Samuel P. Walker. Brought to Memphis in 1851.

Jack Hill: owned by Bolton, Dickens and Co. Sent to G.L. Bumpass of Lexington, Kentucky, on November 18, 1856.

Jack Johnson: owned by Bolton, Dickens and Co. and sold to Murfield on January 8, 1857.

Jacob: about twenty-four years old. "Pursuant to a decree of the Chancery Court at Memphis, rendered at the November term, 1858, in the case of Lucy W. Stark, administratrix of Henry C. Stark, deceased, and others, vs. Margaret Stark, Louisiana Farabee, and others, creditors of Henry C. Stark, deceased, I will on Thursday, the 25th of January, 1859, at the late residence of Henry C. Stark, deceased, in Shelby county, Tennessee, near Fisherville, proceed to sell to the highest bidder." Clerk and master John C. Lanier.

Jacob: arrested for "stealing chickens" on January 10, 1859. Owned by Jack Williams.

Jacob: arrested on December 22, 1858, for "fighting a white man." Owned by C.W. Cherry.

Jacob alias Tom: arrested on May 30, 1859, for being a "runaway slave; thief." Owned by Carter Sowett.

James: "dark complexion, 5 feet 6 or 8 inches tall, weighed about 150 pounds." Owned by Mr. Marshall of Hinds County, Mississippi. Arrested by the Shelby County sheriff for being a runaway slave on December 1, 1839.

James: "20 years old, 5 feet 8 or 10 inches tall, dark complexion." Owned by Mr. McGuire of Giles County, Tennessee. Arrested by the Shelby County sheriff on May 8, 1839, for being a runaway slave.

James Day: arrested on March 21, 1859, for being a runaway. "Dark copper color; 5 feet 8 or 9 inches high; will weigh 155 or 160 pounds; says he is part Indian; no flesh marks visible." Owned by George Torry of Jefferson County, Mississippi.

Jane: a mulatto girl, aged about twelve or thirteen years. Owned by Thomas Bowling, Robert Gee and Eliza Mason and sold to Britton Duke on June 1, 1836.

Jane: thirteen years old, owned by Byrd Hill and Son and sold to L.P.C. Burford on April 1, 1856.

Jane Burns: owned by Bolton, Dickens and Co. Sent to G.L. Bumpass of Lexington, Kentucky, on November 18, 1856.

Jane Kesson: owned by Bolton, Dickens and Co. and sold to Hodge on December 6, 1856.

Jane Nunn: born in Virginia in 1801 and came to Memphis in 1862.

Jane Sneed: about thirty-eight years old in 1866.

Jasper: arrested for "no pass" on November 29, 1859. Owned by Dr. Butts.

Jasper: owned by Bolton, Dickens and Co. and sold to Saul Hawkins of Vicksburg, Mississippi, on September 24, 1856.

Jeff: arrested on November 29, 1860, for "misdemeanor; out on check forfeit." Owned by Kortrecht.

Jefferson: arrested on April 19, 1859. "Says master taking him off to sell." Owned by James Medcaff of Alabama.

Jemima: thirty-three-year-old cook with two children, nine-year-old Levi and twelve-year-old Isabel. Available for hire from January 10, 1859, to January 1, 1860. Owned by M.C. Cayce.

Jenny Lind: about five years old. "Pursuant to a decree of the Chancery Court at Memphis, rendered at the November term, 1858, in the case of Lucy W. Stark, administratrix of Henry C. Stark, deceased, and others, vs. Margaret Stark, Louisiana Farabee, and others, creditors of Henry C. Stark, deceased, I will on Thursday, the 25th of January, 1859, at the late residence of Henry C. Stark, deceased, in Shelby county, Tennessee, near Fisherville, proceed to sell to the highest bidder." Clerk and master John C. Lanier.

Jerry: about thirty years old. "Pursuant to a decree of Chancery Court, at Memphis, rendered November term 1858, in the case of Newton Ford, Administrator of Thomas Mull, deceased, and others, vs. John S. Clayton and others, creditors of Thomas Mull, deceased, I will on Tuesday February 1, 1859, in front of my office, in the City of Memphis, proceed to sell to the highest bidder, for cash." Clerk and master John C. Lanier.

Jerry: "$50 reward will be paid for the apprehension of a dark mulatto slave… who escaped from the depot of the Memphis and Charlotte Railroad, on the night of the 7th. Hight about 6 feet. Had locked to his right leg a pair of shackles, his left leg being swollen. Wore dark-colored clothes. He is owned in Cleveland, Tenn." From an advertisement placed in the *Memphis Daily Appeal* on January 14, 1859, by B. Ayres, superintendent of the Memphis and Charleston Railroad.

Jessie Moon: owned by Bolton, Dickens and Co. Sent to G.L. Bumpass of Lexington, Kentucky, on November 18, 1856.

Jiles: arrested on May 29, 1859, for "gambling with Bob Fulkes." Owned by J. Stratton.

Jim: arrested on December 25, 1858, for "very drunk Christmas spree." Owned by John Wildberger.

Jim: between twenty-five and thirty years old, about five feet ten inches tall. "Has six toes on each foot with a scar on each hand caused by cutting one finger on each hand. Also, a scar on one side of his face caused by a bite; a little inclined to be knock-kneed." Ran away from Claiborne Barksdale on February 27, 1839.

Jim Bealert: owned by Bolton, Dickens and Co. and sold to G.W. Babcock.

Jim Brown: about fifteen years old. "Pursuant to a decree of the Chancery Court at Memphis, rendered at the November term, 1858, in the case of Lucy W. Stark, administratrix of Henry C. Stark, deceased, and others, vs. Margaret Stark, Louisiana Farabee, and others, creditors of Henry C. Stark, deceased, I will on Thursday, the 25th of January, 1859, at the late residence of Henry C. Stark, deceased, in Shelby county, Tennessee, near Fisherville, proceed to sell to the highest bidder." Clerk and master John C. Lanier.

Jim Fedler: owned by Bolton, Dickens and Co. and sold to Hawkins on December 19, 1856.

Jim Gray: about fifteen years old. "Pursuant to a decree of the Chancery Court at Memphis, rendered at the November term, 1858, in the case of Lucy W. Stark, administratrix of Henry C. Stark, deceased, and others, vs. Margaret Stark, Louisiana Farabee, and others, creditors of Henry C.

Stark, deceased, I will on Thursday, the 25th of January, 1859, at the late residence of Henry C. Stark, deceased, in Shelby county, Tennessee, near Fisherville, proceed to sell to the highest bidder." Clerk and master John C. Lanier.

Jim Sikes: owned by Bolton, Dickens and Co. and sold to Duffy on January 23, 1857.

J.M. Horton: owned by A.K. Ward. After emancipation, he owned land and became wealthy in the rural Shelby County community of Cuba.

Joe: forty years old. Field hand. Available for hire from January 10, 1859, to January 1, 1860. Owned by M.C. Cayce.

Joe: owned by Marmaduke Duke.

Joe: "useful servant 12 years old." Sold by J.E. Phillips in front of the Commercial Hotel on February 19, 1846.

Joe McKitchen: owned by Bolton, Dickens and Co. and sold to Murfield on January 8, 1857.

Joe Measley: owned by Bolton, Dickens and Co. and sent by J. Guest.

Joe Nelson: owned by Bolton, Dickens and Co. Sent to Memphis but not sold.

Joe Armstrong Reese: owned by Bolton, Dickens and Co. and sold to Murfield on January 8, 1857.

Joe Richards: owned by Bolton, Dickens and Co. and sold to Murfield on January 8, 1857.

Joe Wilson: owned by Bolton, Dickens and Co. and sent by J. Guest.

John: about twenty years old, five feet, eight inches tall, weighed about 150 pounds and dark brown complexion. Ran away from Mr. Kilpatrick in New Orleans. Arrested as a runaway slave on March 15, 1838, and sold by the Shelby County sheriff on May 1, 1839.

John: arrested for being a runaway on March 17, 1859. "About 23 or 24 years old, 5 feet 6 inches high, weighs about 150 or 160 pounds." Owned by William Rutherford of New Orleans.

John: arrested on November 15, 1858, for being "drunk on the street." Owned by Thomas Mull.

John: "brought to be whipped" at police station on March 31, 1859. Owned by C.C. Clures.

John: "fast driving; sleep on hack." Arrested on August 26, 1860. Owned by Dr. Parrot.

John: "a No. 1 field hand, 26 years old, weighs 180 pounds." Husband of Lucinda. Owned by J.M. Alexander and put up for sale on December 29, 1859.

John: ran away from C. Speigel on April 5, 1859. "Aged about 22 years, of copper color, and 5 feet 8 inches high, more or less flat nose, and large eyes; wears a little moustache."

John: ran away from Germantown, Shelby County, Tennessee, on July 10, 1843. "About 25 years of age, six feet high. John is a very sensible negro, and of good manners—is fond of telling extravagant tales for the amusement of those that are present; he professes to be a barber. He has a smooth skin and of good countenance; he took with him a green frock coat of summer cloth; also, a dress coat of light figured stuff, and a pair of blue cloth pants—other clothing not recollected. No doubt but that he will try to get to some one of the free States." Owned by William Winfrey.

John: ran away from Henry T. Hulbert on June 4, 1859. "He is about five feet ten inches high, black complexion, weighs about 150 pounds, thin visage, very smart, and thirty years of age."

John Blake: owned by Bolton, Dickens and Co. and sold to Murfield on January 8, 1857.

John Braden: owned by Bolton, Dickens and Co. Sent to G.L. Bumpass of Lexington, Kentucky, on December 18, 1856.

John Bull: owned by Bolton, Dickens and Co. Sent to G.L. Bumpass of Lexington, Kentucky, on November 18, 1856.

John Gorden: owned by Bolton, Dickens and Co. and sold to Duffy on January 23, 1857.

John Handy: "freed by Massa Lincoln."

John Hannibal: arrested in Obion County, Tennessee, on September 16, 1859, for running away from William Bradford of Memphis. "About six feet high, weighs about 180 lbs, has a scar over the left eye and one on his right hand caused by a burn, and appears to be about 21 years old."

John Henry: sixteen months old. Son of Marium. Owned by Bolton, Dickens and Co. and sold to Samuel B. Williamson on October 5, 1846.

John Marshall: brought to Memphis in 1861.

John Ruffle: owned by Thomas Dickens and sold to Bolton, Dickens and Co. on February 9, 1857.

John Vaughn: owned by Bolton, Dickens and Co. Sent to G.L. Bumpass of Lexington, Kentucky, on December 18, 1856.

Julia Williams: owned by Bolton, Dickens and Co. Sent to G.L. Bumpass of Lexington, Kentucky, on November 18, 1856.

Jumac: owned by Thomas Dickens and sold to Bolton, Dickens and Co. on February 9, 1857.

Kelly: "house negro" sent to Memphis by Jack Guest on April 23, 1857.

Kemp: arrested on November 20, 1858, for "stealing box fine shoes" and on June 30, 1860, for "attempt to rape." Owned by Greenlaw.

Kit Horne: owned by Thomas P. Horne. Father of Henry and Willis Horne.

Kitty: arrested for "stealing money" on January 28, 1860. Owned by Mr. Nox. Aydelet, agent.

Lacy: arrested for "driving on sidewalk; $25 bail" on October 5, 1860. Owned by G.W. Fisher.

Lafayett: arrested on December 24, 1860, for "misdemeanor." Owned by Henry Brage.

Laree: "put up for safe keeping" on November 24, 1860. Owned by W.B. Richman.

Latisha: "working in city without license" on November 13, 1860. Owned by Donelson.

Lawson: arrested on December 26, 1858, for "concealing runaway slave Mandy; had money." Owned by E.W. Winston.

Lawson: owned by Bolton, Dickens and Co. and sold to Duffy on January 23, 1857.

Lewis: arrested for "no pass; escaped jail; had $3.85" on February 13, 1859, and June 3, 1860, for "no pass." Owned by Gayoso House.

Lewis: ran away from owner Miles W. Goolsley on November 6, 1835. "About 25 years old, about five feet high, pale black, appears very humble when spoken to, speaks low, had on homemade clothing. I think said boy is lurking in the neighborhood of Portersville or Randolph, as I purchased him of John Polk, of Portersville; if not, he is aiming up the river."

Lewis York: owned by Thomas Dickens and sold to Bolton, Dickens and Co. on February 9, 1857.

Leyan: "stole $500 on Memphis-Charleston Railroad." Arrested on November 6, 1860. No owner given.

Lizza: owned by Bolton, Dickens and Co. Sent to G.L. Bumpass of Lexington, Kentucky, on the steamer *Princess* on October 24, 1856.

Lizzie Yellow Girl: owned by Bolton, Dickens and Co. Received from Memphis.

London: owned by Bolton, Dickens and Co. Sent to G.L. Bumpass of Lexington, Kentucky, on the steamer *Princess* on October 24, 1856.

Lucinda: "36 years old, No. 1 Cook and Washer, and four likely children from 20 months to 11 years old." Wife of John. Owned by J.M. Alexander and put up for sale on December 29, 1859.

Lucy: four years old. Sold at auction to A.C. Treadwell in 1858.

Lucy: thirty-two-year-old seamstress and cook. Available for hire from January 10, 1859, to January 1, 1860. Owned by M.C. Cayce.

Malinda: sold by auctioneer J.E. Phillips on March 11, 1846, at the Commercial Hotel.

Malinda and her child: owned by Bolton, Dickens and Co. and sold to Hodge on December 6, 1856.

Manah Hayse: owned by Bolton, Dickens and Co. Sent to G.L. Bumpass of Lexington, Kentucky, on November 18, 1856.

March: "dark copper color, 26 or 27 years of age, 5 feet 9 or 10 inches high, tolerably stout built, will weigh about 160 pounds and has several scars or welts on his breast. He is a shrewd smart fellow, and will no doubt tell a plausible tale if apprehended. He has a limp or halt in his walk as if one of his legs was shorter than the other. I purchased the negro of George S. Fogleman of Arkansas in March 1844. Fogleman purchased him of H.B.H. Williams, living on Yellow Creek, Dickson County, Tennessee." Owned by Charles Jones and ran away on July 1, 1845.

Marcus: arrested on November 23, 1860, for being "drunk; a wood hauler." Owned by Louis Whit.

Margaret: age thirty, no. 1 house servant. Owned by A. Wallace.

Marguerite: two years old. Sold by J.E. Phillips in front of the Commercial Hotel on February 19, 1846.

Mariah: on March 30, 1859, "brought to be whipped by [policeman] Smith." Owned by Mrs. McClure.

Martha: about seventeen years old. "Speaks fluently when spoken to, but easily confused when conversing with her." Ran away from William A. Jones on February 11, 1839.

Martha: age about sixteen months. Daughter of Susan. Emancipated in 1850.

Martha: arrested on May 14, 1860, for "no pass." Owned by William Taylor.

Martha: infant. Deed of trust issued in 1850.

Martha: owned by Bolton, Dickens and Co. Received from Memphis.

Martha: ran away from William A. Jones on February 11, 1839. "A dark mulatto girl…about seventeen years of age, speaks fluently when spoken to, but is easily confused in conversing with her."

Martin: arrested on May 31, 1859, for being a "runaway or hired to Captain Bowman." "Sent home to master."

Mary: about thirty-three years old. "Pursuant to a decree of the Chancery Court at Memphis, rendered at the November term, 1858, in the case of Lucy W. Stark, administratrix of Henry C. Stark, deceased, and others, vs. Margaret Stark, Louisiana Farabee, and others, creditors of Henry C. Stark, deceased, I will on Thursday, the 25th of January, 1859, at the late residence of Henry C. Stark, deceased, in Shelby county, Tennessee, near Fisherville, proceed to sell to the highest bidder."

Mary: age sixteen, no. 1 cook, washer and ironer. Owned by A. Wallace.

Mary: eight years old. Member of a "likely family of Negroes." Auctioned by A.S. Levy and Company on April 28, 1859.

Mary: "excellent general hand, 9 years old." Sold by J.E. Phillips in front of the Commercial Hotel on February 19, 1846.

Mary: fifteen years old, dark complexion. Sold by Forrest and Maples to S.H. Davis on September 29, 1855.

Mary: thirty-seven years old on January 14, 1859. "The Corporation charging more than I am able to pay for license, having been totally raised to about eight hundred dollars, including auction and negro license, brought forward by one of our city fathers in the same business as myself, so I have been told, but it is immaterial who was the originator of the outrageous tax, I for one, cannot pay it, therefore I wish to change my business, and will sell all the negroes on hand low for cash."

Mary: twenty-three-year-old housekeeper and cook. Available for hire from January 10, 1859, to January 1, 1860. Owned by M.C. Cayce.

Mary Ann: about twenty-one years old. "Pursuant to a decree of the Chancery Court at Memphis, rendered at the November term, 1858, in the case of Lucy W. Stark, administratrix of Henry C. Stark, deceased, and others, vs. Margaret Stark, Louisiana Farabee, and others, creditors of Henry C. Stark, deceased, I will on Thursday, the 25th of January, 1859, at the late residence of Henry C. Stark, deceased, in Shelby county, Tennessee, near Fisherville, proceed to sell to the highest bidder." Clerk and master John C. Lanier.

Mary Ashley: owned by Bolton, Dickens and Co. Sent to G.L. Bumpass of Lexington, Kentucky, on November 18, 1856.

Mary Baker: owned by Bolton, Dickens and Co. and sold to Duffy on January 23, 1857.

Mary Brown: owned by Bolton, Dickens and Co. and sold to Hawkins on December 19, 1856.

Mary Farancis: owned by Bolton, Dickens and Co. and sold to Hawkins on December 19, 1856.

Melinda: ten years old. Sold by James J. Baugh, administrator of the estate of Josiah Baugh, on March 11, 1846.

Melvin: "wrongly discharged by mayor" on March 8, 1859. Owned by W. Vance.

Milley and her three children: owned by Bolton, Dickens and Co. and sold to Saul Hawkins of Vicksburg, Mississippi, on September 24, 1856.

Milly: about ten years old. Sold at auction by Thomas Mull to A.C. Treadwell in 1858.

Milly: infant. Deed of trust issued in 1850.

Milton: arrested on July 21, 1859, for being "without pass." Owned by the Davis Steamboat.

Mitch: "aged about forty years, of yellow complexion about six-foot-high and rotund in his appearance." Owned by Lawrence H. Bedford. Ran away on May 5, 1836.

Mitchell: arrested for being a runaway "entertaining his wife" on July 11, 1859. Owned by Mrs. Cox.

Molly Bill: owned by Bolton, Dickens and Co. Sent to G.L. Bumpass of Lexington, Kentucky, on November 18, 1856.

Moses: "drove dray on pavement." Arrested on February 12, 1859. Owned by Mrs. Bibee.

Moses: good general hand, twenty-two years old. Sold by J.E. Phillips in front of the Commercial Hotel on February 19, 1846.

Moses Clark: owned by Bolton, Dickens and Co.

Muslen Vance: owned by Bolton, Dickens and Co. Sent to G.L. Bumpass of Lexington, Kentucky, on November 18, 1856.

Nancy: about sixteen years old, dark complexion, weighed about 190 pounds. Owned by William Owens of Brownsville, Tennessee. Arrested by the Shelby County sheriff for being a runaway slave on January 13, 1840.

Nancy: eight years old, a member of a "likely family of Negroes." Auctioned by A.S. Levy and Company on April 28, 1859.

Nancy and her three children: sold by clerk and master John C. Lanier on August 1, 1859. "Pursuant to a decree of the Chancery Court at Memphis, rendered May term, 1859, in the case of William Braswell and Mary Braswell vs. Benjamin Askew and D.M. Sanders, upon the ex parte petition of Wm. L. Braswell and wife, Elizabeth Braswell…as the property of the petitioner, Elizabeth Braswell."

Ned: ran away in May 1859. "Formerly owned by Mrs. Tucker. He is described as being of a dark brown color, about forty-five or fifty years old, and as being smart and sly. He has worked about the city, and may be still lurking around; but it is more probable that he has gone off, perhaps to a free State in company with John, who belongs to the same estate." Executor J.H. Unthank, attorney in fact for Mrs. M. Blount Williams.

Nicy Hines: owned by Bolton, Dickens and Co. and sold to Hodge on December 6, 1856.

Novel: seventeen years old, five feet nine inches tall, yellow complexion, weighs about 130 pounds. Owned by William Event of Vicksburg, Mississippi. Arrested for being a runaway slave by the Shelby County sheriff on October 25, 1839.

Pall: about thirty years old, "quite black," five feet four or five inches tall, weighed about 130 pounds. Arrested by the Shelby County sheriff for being a runaway slave on October 17, 1839.

Past Ann: owned by Bolton, Dickens and Co.

Patrick Henry: owned by John T. Nelson and sold to Britton Duke in January 1842.

Paul: arrested on July 13, 1843, for being a runaway. "A dark copper colour, 5 feet 8 inches high; will weigh 165 lbs., about 22 years old, has a scar in the forehead over the right eye, and one on the right hand, starting at the last joint of the middle finger and terminating about half way between the last joint of the little finger and wrist; he cannot straighten the little finger of either hand." Owned by John Gordon of LaGrange, Tennessee.

Paul: "of common size, dark color, 5 feet 8 or 10 inches high, 21 or 22 years old, had on boots when he left." Owned by the Carey family and sold to I.P.C. Burford of DeSoto County, Mississippi. Ran away on March 1, 1840.

Peter: about fifty-one years old, five feet, ten inches tall, weighed about 165 pounds. Owned by Jenny May of Fayette County, Tennessee. Arrested by the Shelby County sheriff for being a runaway slave on January 13, 1840.

Peter: "a boy about 40 or 45 years of age, 5 feet 3 or 4 inches high, weighs about 144, very black, little bald headed, a tooth out before." Owned by Stephen Rutlan of DeSoto County, Mississippi. Arrested by the Shelby County sheriff for being a runaway slave on March 23, 1840.

Peter: arrested for being a runaway on September 19, 1843. "A light complexted negro, about 22 years old, 5 feet 7 inches high, will weigh 140 lbs, and has a small scar in the forehead." Owned by Major Story of Carroll County, Mississippi.

Peter Ingram: owned by Bolton, Dickens and Co. Sent to Memphis by Wade Bolton on March 24, 1857.

Phillip: twenty-five years old on January 14, 1859. "The Corporation charging more than I am able to pay for license, having been totally raised to about eight hundred dollars, including auction and negro license, brought forward by one of our city fathers in the same business as myself, so I have been told, but it is immaterial who was the originator of the outrageous tax, I for one, cannot pay it, therefore I wish to change my business, and will sell all the Negroes on hand low for cash."

Pleasant: ran away from Patrick Meagher on October 26, 1827. "A negro man aged about 30 years, of common size and pretty well built; is soft spoken, but somewhat impudent when in liquor, to which he is addicted on some occasions dresses fine, and with more than ordinary neatness, which gives an air of consequence which he does not commonly assume."

Port Ann: owned by Bolton, Dickens and Co. Sent to G.L. Bumpass of Lexington, Kentucky, on December 18, 1856.

Quicksel, also known as Cato: "he is a stout black man, speaks soft, a pleasing countenance, and is likely passing himself for a free man and probably calls himself Cato." Ran away on February 19, 1839.

Rachael and her child: owned by Bolton, Dickens and Co. and sold to Murfield on January 8, 1857.

Rachael Carr: owned by cotton merchant Harlow Dow. Lived with Judge L.B. McFarland in 1916.

Rachel: "excellent general hand 30 years old." Sold by J.E. Phillips in front of the Commercial Hotel on February 19, 1846.

Rachel Tumble: owned by Bolton, Dickens and Co. Sent to G.L. Bumpass of Lexington, Kentucky, on November 18, 1856.

Rebeca: a child. Deed of trust in 1850.

Rebecca: about fourteen years old. Sold by Thomas Mull to D.H. Hull in 1858.

Rebecca: owned by Bolton, Dickens and Co. and sold to Saul Hawkins of Vicksburg, Mississippi, on September 24, 1856.

Reed: arrested on March 3, 1859, for "working without a pass; no money." Owned by Thomas Beard.

Reuben: about twenty years old, five feet, eight or ten inches tall, weighed about 140 pounds. Ran away from Mr. Polk in Holly Springs, Mississippi, and arrested as a runaway slave on April 7, 1839.

Robert: "a likely yellow fellow, 21 or 22 years of age, about 5 feet ten inches high, has a scar on his right hand, occasioned by a burn. Robert is very stout, weighs about 180 pounds." Owned by Durritt and Barnes, ran away on September 30, 1836.

Robert: "gambling & caught in the act" with Jiles on May 29, 1859. Owned by P. Fulkes.

Robert: "runaway from his farm; to jail." Arrested on April 30, 1859. Owned by Dr. A.P. Merrell.

Robert: owned by Bolton, Dickens and Co. and sold to Saul Hawkins of Vicksburg, Mississippi, on September 24, 1856.

Robert: arrested for "going in drinking house" on August 11, 1859. Owned by Cockrel.

Robert: owned by Bolton, Dickens and Co. Sent to G.L. Bumpass of Lexington, Kentucky, on the steamer *Princess* on October 24, 1856.

Robert Lewis: owned by Bolton, Dickens and Co. and sold to Hodge on December 6, 1856.

Robert Henry Lewis: owned by Bolton, Dickens and Co. and sold to Murfield on January 8, 1857.

Robin Farm: owned by Bolton, Dickens and Co. and sold to G.W. Babcock.

Robsen Cleveland: owned by Bolton, Dickens and Co. Sent to G.L. Bumpass of Lexington, Kentucky, on November 18, 1856.

Rozetta: two years old. Sold by J.E. Phillips in front of the Commercial Hotel on February 19, 1846.

Sally and her child: sold by James J. Baugh, administrator of the estate of Josiah Baugh, on March 11, 1846.

Sally Fugon: owned by Bolton, Dickens and Co.

Sam: sold at auction by G.B. Locke and Company on May 28, 1859. "40 years old, a good Blacksmith."

Sampson Dunn: owned by Bolton, Dickens and Co. and sold to G.W. Babcock.

Sandy: ran away from owner Miles W. Goolsley on October 29, 1835. "Has had the scald head which makes his hair very thin. I suppose he will aim for Memphis or Randolph and endeavor to get on a boat going up the river."

Sara Elizabeth: owned by Bolton, Dickens and Co.

Sarah: "good cook, washer, ironer, &c, 23 years old." Sold by J.E. Phillips in front of the Commercial Hotel on February 19, 1846.

Sarah Bull: owned by Bolton, Dickens and Co. Sent to G.L. Bumpass of Lexington, Kentucky, on November 18, 1856.

Sarah Cubbin: owned by Bolton, Dickens and Co.

Sarah Forrester: owned by Bolton, Dickens and Co. Sent to G.L. Bumpass of Lexington, Kentucky, on November 18, 1856.

Sarah Frances: owned by Bolton, Dickens and Co. and sold to Hawkins on December 19, 1856.

Sarah Green: wife of Solomon Green.

Sarah Grimes: owned by Bolton, Dickens and Co. and sent by J. Guest.

Sarah Martel: owned by Bolton, Dickens and Co. and sent by J. Guest.

Scy: about thirty-five years old. "Pursuant to a decree of Chancery Court, at Memphis, rendered November term 1858, in the case of Newton Ford, Administrator of Thomas Mull, deceased, and others, vs. John S. Clayton and others, creditors of Thomas Mull, deceased, I will on Tuesday February 1, 1859, in front of my office, in the City of Memphis, proceed to sell to the highest bidder, for cash." Clerk and master John C. Lanier.

Silas Carter: owned by Bolton, Dickens and Co. Sent to G.L. Bumpass of Lexington, Kentucky, on November 18, 1856.

Soloman: arrested on January 3, 1860, for "fast driving; decently whipt." Arrested on February 16, 1860, for "misdemeanor; locked up before Recorder." Arrested for being "without pass" on February 17, 1860, and "a runaway; sent to jail" on May 20, 1860. Owned by Grider.

Stephen: arrested on September 28, 1843, for being a runaway "tolerably black, about 27 years old, will weigh 160 lbs., is 5 feet 9¼ inches high, small scar in the right eyebrow, the last joint of the ring finger of the left hand has been hurt, the end of the finger turns up, scar from a burn on the back of the right hand, also a scar from a burn on the right arm below the elbow, the elbow joint of the left arm has been hurt, and the arm will not straighten." Owned by Dr. Lee of Marshall County, Mississippi.

Stephen Bale: owned by Bolton, Dickens and Co.

Stephen Garrett: owned by Bolton, Dickens and Co. Sent to G.L. Bumpass of Lexington, Kentucky, on November 18, 1856.

Susan: eight years old. Sold by J.E. Phillips in front of the Commercial Hotel on February 19, 1846.

Susan: three years old. Sold by J.E. Phillips in front of the Commercial Hotel on February 19, 1846.

Susan Hays: owned by General Hays.

Taylor: ran away from J.M.M. Cornelius of Germantown, Shelby County, Tennessee, on October 2, 1860. "A small, well-set, black negro with one leg a little shorter than the other, small round eyes, and a very small receding chin, so much that he has very nearly no chin."

Taylor Hunt: coachman for Mr. Davis. Age sixteen years old.

Thomas Bradshaw: about forty-eight years old in 1866. Barber and musician. Owned by Mr. Bradshaw. Brought to Memphis around 1846.

Thompson: thirty-seven years old, five feet, five inches tall, dark complexion. Owned by James Watson of Missouri. Arrested for being a runaway and held in the Shelby County Jail on September 18, 1838. Sold by Shelby County sheriff on October 7, 1839.

Tim No. 3: owned by Marmaduke Duke.

Tom: about twenty-eight years old. "Pursuant to a decree of Chancery Court, at Memphis, rendered November term 1858, in the case of Newton Ford, Administrator of Thomas Mull, deceased, and others, vs. John S. Clayton and others, creditors of Thomas Mull, deceased, I will on Tuesday February 1, 1859, in front of my office, in the City of Memphis, proceed to sell to the highest bidder, for cash." Clerk and master John C. Lanier.

Tom: twenty-five years old, five feet eight or ten inches tall, 140 pounds, dark brown complexion. Owned by James Woods of Hardeman County, Tennessee. Arrested for being a runaway slave on March 21, 1840, by the Shelby County sheriff.

Tom Bar: owned by Bolton, Dickens and Co. and sold to Saul Hawkins of Vicksburg, Mississippi, on September 24, 1856.

Tom Robert: owned by Bolton, Dickens and Co. and sold to Saul Hawkins of Vicksburg, Mississippi, on September 24, 1856.

Toney: arrested on October 29, 1860, for fighting. Owned by William Walker.

Travis: "quick spoken with a scar below his eye from a burn, was well paddled before he left." Owned by N.R. Sledge.

Turner: arrested on October 8, 1860, "said to be drunk; had 50 cents." Owned by R.K. Turmery.

Tyler: arrested on November 8, 1860, "tax not paid; but was paid." Owned by Williamson.

Tyrous: arrested for "no pass" on November 13, 1859. Owned by Mrs. Looney.

Viney: owned by Marmaduke Duke.

Violet: three years old. A member of a "likely family of Negroes." Auctioned by A.S. Levy and Company on April 28, 1859.

Washington: arrested on October 10, 1860, for "living contrary to law; $25 bail." Owned by Thomas Sanderson.

Watt: arrested "without pass" on January 21, 1860. Owned by E.V. Trezevant.

Wesley: about thirty-four years old. Sold by Thomas Mull to D.L. Childress.

Wesley: indicted for murder in 1851.

Wesley: owned by Bolton, Dickens and Co.

West: "put in for safe keeping; had $7" on December 17, 1859. Owned by John Martin.

Westly: owned by Bolton, Dickens and Co.

Wilbourne: about twenty-four years old. Owned by George Farley and sold to Samuel B. Williamson.

Will: "arrested; had knife" on August 27, 1859. Owned by Sam Woodson.

William: about twenty-six years old. Owned by Patrick H. McCutchen and sold to Samuel B. Williamson on June 30, 1846.

William: arrested for gambling on October 9, 1858. Owned by W. Ferguson.

William: arrested on May 2, 1859, "drunk with his dray & disorderly." Owned by Dubose.

William: arrested on November 13, 1843, for being a runaway. "A yellow man, 5 feet 7¼ inches high, about 25 years old, will weigh 170 lbs., one upper front tooth missing." Owned by John Elliot of Stanton, Augusta County, Virginia.

William: "dark complected, about 23 years old, heavy built, will weigh about 160 pounds, wears rings in his ears, slightly knock-kneed. He is supposed to be about Memphis, or in Arkansas in the neighborhood of DesArc." Ran away on December 23, 1859. Owned by William H. Weller.

William: owned by Bolton, Dickens and Co.

William: twenty-seven years old, dark complexion, 160 pounds, five feet, eight or ten inches tall. Owned by Bird Crawley of Coffeeville, Mississippi. Arrested as a runaway slave by the Shelby County sheriff on March 10, 1840.

William Bande: owned by Bolton, Dickens and Co. and sold to Hodge on December 6, 1856.

William B. Smith: owned by Bolton, Dickens and Co. and sold to Hodge on December 6, 1856.

William Coe: blacksmith in 1866.

William Gaskins: owned by Bolton, Dickens and Co. and sold to Saul Hawkins of Vicksburg, Mississippi, on September 24, 1856.

William Henry: owned by Bolton, Dickens and Co. and sent by J. Guest.

William Johnson: owned by Bolton, Dickens and Co.

William Wright: owned by Bolton, Dickens and Co.

Willis: about nineteen years old, yellow complexion, five feet, eight inches tall, weighed about 123 pounds. Owned by William Collier. Arrested by the Shelby County sheriff for being a runaway slave on January 31, 1840.

Willis: "good general hand 25 years old." Sold by J.E. Phillips in front of the Commercial Hotel on February 19, 1846.

Willis: twenty-five years old, six feet tall, "very black," 180 pounds. Owned by David Henderson of Holly Springs, Mississippi. Arrested for being a runaway slave by the Shelby County sheriff on March 10, 1840.

Willis Hodges: owned by Mrs. W.R. Hunt. Died on December 29, 1897.

Willis Horne: owned by Thomas P. Horne. Brother of Henry and son of Kit Horne.

Woodsen Smith: owned by Bolton, Dickens and Co. and sold to G.W. Babcock.

York: arrested on February 5, 1860, for "fighting; turned out by order of Captain Garrett; $25." Owned by Mrs. Carrall.

Zack: "sent to jail" on October 10, 1858. Owned by W. Richards.

Zuene: arrested for "disorderly conduct" on July 15, 1859. Owned by Feryanson.

SOURCES

Articles

Eiland, Sarah. "The Unspoken Demands of Slavery: The Exploitation of Female Slaves in the Memphis Slave Trade." *Rhodes Historical Review* 20 (Spring 2018).

Huebner, Timothy S. "Making History Public in Memphis: Creating a Historical Marker in a Methods Course." *American Historian* (August 2018).

Tilly, Bette B. "The Spirit of Improvement: Reformism and Slavery in West Tennessee." *West Tennessee Historical Society Papers* 38 (1974).

Wall, Austin. "Direct from Congo: Nathan Bedford Forrest's Involvement in the Illegal African Slave Trade." *Rhodes Historical Review* 20 (Spring 2018).

Walters, Rev. Scott. "Something Sacred and True." *Chronicle*, Summer 2018.

Books

Arnebeck, Bob. *Slave Labor in the Capital.* Charleston, SC: The History Press, 2014.

Bancroft, Frederic. *Slave Trading in the Old South.* Columbia: University of South Carolina Press, 1996.

Carriere, Marius, Jr. "Blacks in Pre–Civil War Memphis." In *Trial and Triumph: Essays in Tennessee's African American History* by Carroll Van West. Knoxville: University of Tennessee Press, 2002.

Davis, David Brion. *Inhuman Bondage: The Rise and Fall of Slavery in the New World.* Oxford: Oxford University Press, 2006.

DeClue, Stephanie, and Mary Louise Nazor. *Index of the Shelby County Quarterly Court Records, 1820–1865.* Memphis, TN: History Department, Memphis/Shelby County Public Library and Information Center, 2000.

Hensley, Kenneth. *The Bolton-Dickens Feud: A Statue's Tale.* Pine Bluff, AR: Hensley Publications, 1991.

Huebner, Timothy S. *Liberty and Union: The Civil War Era and American Constitutionalism.* Lawrence: University Press of Kansas, 2016.

Hughes, Louis. *Thirty Years a Slave.* Montgomery, AL: NewSouth Books, 2002.

Hurst, Jack. *Nathan Bedford Forrest: A Biography.* New York: A.A. Knopf, 1993.

Keating, J.M. *History of the City of Memphis and Shelby County, Tennessee.* Syracuse: D. Mason and Co., 1888.

Lauterbach, Preston. *Beale Street Dynasty.* New York: W.W. Norton and Company, Inc., 2015.

Memphis Riots and Massacres, 1866. Miami, FL: Mnemosyne Publishing, Co., Inc., 1969.

Nazor, Mary Louise. *Memphis City Police Station Book, October 1, 1858 to December 30, 1860.* Memphis, TN: Memphis/Shelby County Archives, 1997.

Neely, Shirley C. *Bolton, Dickens & Co. Record of Slaves, 1856–1858.* Memphis, TN: Memphis Public Libraries, 2005.

Olmsted, Frederick Law. *The Cotton Kingdom: A Traveller's Observations on Cotton and Slavery in the American Slave States.* N.p.: Mason Brothers, 1861.

Sigafoos, Robert A. *Cotton Row to Beale Street: A Business History of Memphis.* Memphis, TN: Memphis State University Press, 1979.

Simpson, Brooks D., and Jean V. Berlin, eds. *Sherman's Civil War: Selected Correspondence of William T. Sherman, 1860–1865.* Chapel Hill: University of North Carolina Press, 1999.

Takagi, Midori. *Rearing Wolves to Our Own Destruction: Slavery in Richmond, Virginia, 1782–1865.* Charlottesville: University Press of Virginia, 1999.

Trammell, Jack. *The Richmond Slave Trade.* Charleston, SC: The History Press, 2012.

United States War Department. *Official Record of the War of Rebellion.* Washington, D.C.: Government Printing Office, 1880.

MANUSCRIPT COLLECTIONS

Britton Duke Papers, Memphis and Shelby County Room, Memphis Public Libraries.

Business Papers of Samuel B. Williamson, Napoleon Hill and Noland Fontaine, Memphis and Shelby County Room, Memphis Public Libraries.

Historical and Genealogical Collection, Memphis and Shelby County Room, Memphis Public Libraries.

NEWSPAPER ARTICLES

American Eagle, February 28, 1842; March 25, 1842; May 20, 1842.

Commercial Appeal, February 5, 1895; June 23, 1895; January 29, 1896; April 24, 1896; September 8, 1896; January 3, 1897; September 29, 1897; November 28, 1897; January 16, 1898; November 17, 1898; December 8, 1899; November 9, 1902; June 21, 1905; March 29, 1907; June 13, 1907; July 25, 1908; March 17, 1909; April 6, 1909; May 22, 1909; June 7, 1909; June 13, 1910; June 14, 1910; June 27, 1910; July 22, 1910; February 15, 1911; March 29, 1911; April 20, 1911; July 13, 1911; July 16, 1911; July 17, 1911; August 8, 1911; August 12, 1911; November 7, 1911; November 30, 1914; December 3, 1916; January 21, 1917; January 28, 1917; April 5, 1917; October 25, 1917; March 22, 1918; July 16, 1920; July 2, 1925; December 8, 1925; May 27, 1927; July 31, 1928; August 1, 1928; September 17, 1928; April 14, 1929; August 18, 1929; December 29, 1929; May 24, 1932; July 4, 1932; April 28, 1933; October 1, 1933; April 6, 1934.

Memphis Appeal, January 31, 1888.

Memphis Daily Appeal, January 3, 1857; February 4, 1857; February 18, 1857; March 1, 1857; March 17, 1857; April 19, 1857; April 26, 1857; May 5, 1857; May 31, 1857; August 21, 1857; October 15, 1857; November 25, 1857; December 11, 1857; January 6, 1858; February 7, 1858; February 19, 1858; April 28, 1858; May 26, 1858; June 4, 1858; June 5, 1858; June 9, 1858; June 10, 1858; July 22, 1858; October 21, 1858; October 23, 1858; January 30, 1859; February 1, 1859; February 2, 1859; March 24, 1859; April 22, 1859; May 31, 1859; July 29, 1859; October 11, 1859; February 22, 1860; June 15, 1860; August 1, 1860;

March 3, 1861; April 2, 1861; May 26, 1861; May 31, 1861; June 23, 1861; January 1, 1862; January 7, 1862; January 22, 1862; February 5, 1862; March 4, 1862; March 23, 1862; April 2, 1862; June 3, 1862.

Memphis Enquirer, September 28, 1836; October 7, 1837; September 18, 1838; October 26, 1838; November 2, 1838; November 23, 1838; November 30, 1838; December 14, 1838; December 28, 1838; February 1, 1839; February 12, 1839; February 22, 1839; March 1, 1839; March 8, 1839; March 15, 1839; March 22, 1839; March 29, 1839; May 3, 1839; May 24, 1839; June 21, 1839; June 28, 1839; July 26, 1839; August 23, 1839; September 20, 1839; October 11, 1839; November 8, 1839; November 19, 1839; November 25, 1839; December 3, 1839; December 6, 1839; December 20, 1839; January 31, 1840; February 7, 1840; February 21, 1840; March 6, 1840; March 13, 1840; March 27, 1840; April 10, 1840; April 17, 1840; April 24, 1840; May 8, 1840; June 2, 1840; June 5, 1840.

Memphis Union Appeal, July 8, 1862; July 10, 1862; July 18, 1862; August 9, 1862; August 19, 1862.

Randolph Recorder, September 25, 1835; November 6, 1835.

Tri-Weekly Appeal, January 1, 1846; January 22, 1846; January 27, 1846; February 14, 1846; February 24, 1846; March 3, 1846; March 12, 1846; March 14, 1846; March 26, 1846; April 7, 1846; August 29, 1846; September 29, 1846; November 10, 1846; May 4, 1847.

Other Sources

Bond, Beverly Greene. "'Till Fair Aurora Rise': African American Women in Memphis, Tennessee, 1840–1915." PhD dissertation, University of Memphis, 1996.

Cimprich, John Vincent, Jr. "Slavery Amidst Civil War in Tennessee: The Death of an Institution." PhD dissertation, The Ohio State University, 1977.

Federal Writers' Project. *Slave Narratives: A Folk History of Slavery in the United States from Interviews with Former Slaves, 1836–1938*. Washington, D.C.: Works Projects Administration, 1941.

Memphis City directories.

Runaway Slave Blog. Compiled by Naomi Van Tol. spiny.com/runaway.
Sampson, Shereen. "Reclaiming a Historic Landscape: The Interpretation of Frances Wright's Nashoba Plantation in Germantown, Tennessee." Master's thesis, Middle Tennessee State University, December 1998.

INDEX

J

K

L

M

R

S

T

W

ABOUT THE AUTHOR

G. Wayne Dowdy is the senior manager of the Memphis Public Libraries history department. He holds a master's degree in history from the University of Arkansas. Dowdy is a contributing writer for the *Best Times* magazine and *Storyboard Memphis*. He is the author of seven books, including *A Brief History of Memphis*, *Hidden History of Memphis*, *Lost Restaurants of Memphis* and *On This Day in Memphis History*, which was awarded a Certificate of Merit by the Tennessee Historical Commission.